A Mother's Heartbreak: How Scientology Destroyed My Family

By Lori Hodgson

Book Publishers Network
P.O. Box 2256
Bothell • WA • 98041
Ph • 425-483-3040
www.bookpublishersnetwork.com

10 9 8 7 6 5 4 3 2 1
Printed in the United States of America

LCCN 2018935502
ISBN 978-1-945271-95-3

A portion of the proceeds from the sale of this book will go toward efforts to eradicate Scientology's Disconnection Policy.

To my two children so they know the truth and how hard I am fighting to reunite our family. And to all the broken families torn apart by Scientology Disconnection.

NEVER GIVE UP HOPE!

Contents

Introduction

February 6, 2011 is a day that I will never forget. The events haunt me daily as I struggle with the insurmountable anguish and heartbreak of being "disconnected" from my children at the hands of the Church of Scientology. Scientology ripped apart my family. My children, who felt like the very essence of my being, were forced to choose between remaining in contact with me after my resignation from what had been our mutual church, or buying into Scientology's belief system that their eternity would be in jeopardy if they continued communicating with their mother. You see, any former Scientologist who is not "in good standing" with the church will lose their family and friends who are Scientologists through what is known as Scientology disconnection.

I never could have imagined that a religion I once valued would, against my wishes, actively recruit my minor children to work on staff and induct my son into the Sea Organization (a dedicated group within Scientology in which one signs a one-billion-year contract to serve Scientology for this lifetime and future lifetimes as well). Officers of the organization didn't just restrict my contact with them; they forced my son to sign a three-million-dollar gag agreement, silencing him from speaking out about his time within the Sea Org. This meant that if he ever chose to speak out about what he saw or heard when he was in the Sea Org, he would be liable to Scientology for that astonishing amount of money.

Unfortunately, this is my ongoing reality. I have appeared on television shows, including ABC's "20/20", and have given endless interviews, both on television and in print, yet Scientology will not budge. My children remain "disconnected" from me and have been manipulated into believing—no matter what I did for them, no matter how many loving experiences we had together for decades—that I am one of the worst people on the planet, an "anti-Scientologist" and "Suppressive Person."

That is why I am writing this book. My kids were exposed to Scientology because I got involved. I take responsibility for that. I am dedicated, however, to doing everything I can to get my family back together and inform everyone I can what happens to Scientology families if one parent does not agree with what Scientology wants to do with their children! I want everyone to know everything I went through and continue to suffer with daily. My hope is that no other parent has to suffer like I am because of Scientology disconnection. I hope my story helps.

Lori Hodgson

Chapter One

I Wasn't Born into Scientology

I'm beginning with my childhood as it portrays my happy, loving family when I was young and how those strong family values that I had were what was most important to me when I had my own family. The title might seem odd, but several people who have written books about the religion invented by L. Ron Hubbard were born to parents already involved. Not me. Our family was a happy one when I came along on February 8, 1963, as Lori Lynn Moore. My Mom and Dad thought I displayed a "Hello World!" attitude from the beginning. As a baby in my crib, I always seemed to have my head held high and was constantly bobbing around. They quickly nicknamed me "Little Bob-Bob." They couldn't believe their newborn was already attempting to hold her head up to look around.

At three months old, I was baptized Lutheran. My mom was a Sunday school teacher and had also been baptized Lutheran. My faith in God started at a very early age. I remember my childhood years going to Sunday school with my great-grandma. She baby-sat me from time to time and we went to church together on Sunday mornings. Mom and Dad made sure I said my prayers before I went to sleep, and there was a family prayer before supper every night.

In the summer of 1963, my parents bought a lake house in Clear Lake, California. I wasn't even a year old. I spent my childhood summers there at the lake. I was their only child, always on the go, never sitting down to relax. I was a full-time job for my parents, to say the least. I asked my dad "Why?" about everything.

"Dad, why is it cloudy?" "Dad, why is the lake choppy?" That has never stopped; I still ask lots of questions, a quality that got me in trouble later in life, in Scientology.

Dad was a truck driver and my mom was able to stay home with me. Dad would bring us up to the lake on Memorial Day weekend and we would spend the whole summer there until Labor Day. Dad would come up on the weekends. I loved being raised at the lake in the summers. It was a magical place for me. My parents loved it, too.

We were quite a happy little family. I was truly a summer girl who enjoyed lying in the sun, running through the sprinklers, swimming in the lake, and feeding the ducks. Mom used to take me out on the lake in the cove in front of our house. We each had our own inner tubes. She had our poodle Pepi on her tube and I was right next to her, floating around the cove on hot afternoons.

I learned how to water-ski at four years old. I was one of the youngest kids at the lake to get up on water skis. Everyone had big boats that would pull kids over too hard, so my neighbor tried getting me up behind his small fishing boat. I got up the first try; I was so light that I just popped up. I remember getting up and thinking that this was the best thing ever. I absolutely loved water-skiing!

After that, our family went to Library Park to see the hot boat water-ski races. We parked close to the races. A girl with duct tape wrapped around her hands jumped off the bow of her hot boat, grabbed the 100-foot ski rope, and took off with lightning speed. I told my parents,

"When I get big I'm gonna do that!"

They glanced at each other with an "oh boy, are we in trouble!" look. I tended to be more on the adventurous side, but that statement wasn't something so easily accomplished.

Unfortunately, I was born with a smaller left foot and leg. At that time, the doctors had no answers to fix my problem. When I was five, however, a surgeon and his wife moved in next door to us at our Sunnyvale, California, home. The surgeon noticed I was limping and told me I should go see his friend, a specialist at Stanford Hospital. Mom called and got me in to see Dr. Campbell, a well-known orthopedic surgeon. He told my mother that my left leg tendon was too tight and it was hindering the growth of my leg. He said if we didn't do something about it, I would have extreme difficulty later with walking, let alone doing any kind of sports. He mentioned that there was a tendon lengthening surgery that he could do that might help, except the surgery had never been done before. I would be the first one to ever have the surgery. There was also a chance it wouldn't work and that I would be stuck with my leg continuing to be stunted from growth.

I remember overhearing the doctor tell my mother this and I thought to myself, *This surgery will work and I'm going to do all the sports I want to do and be good at them, too.*

After much discussion, my parents decided to go for it and we set up the surgery. I remember I had to have a lot of tests beforehand. One test scared me to death! I remember being in this room and seeing a large pad of needles that they placed on my leg and it hurt like heck. After this last test, the surgery date was only a few weeks away. I was pretty scared about the surgery. I was hoping that my leg operation was not going to be as painful as the tests with those needles. To this day I still don't like needles; maybe this is why. The day of my surgery finally came and I was a scared little girl. My parents consoled me and said it will be all done soon and that I would have a surprise afterward. The surprise kept my mind from worrying so much.

I remember going through the big hospital doors with my parents by my side and then being prepared for surgery. I had to change into a hospital gown. I thought I'd rather be wearing my Batman pajamas. The nurse wheeled me into the operating room and I said goodbye to my parents. Now I was *really* afraid as they put a mask on my face and told me to count to ten, but the next thing I remember I was in a hospital room looking up at my parents. I didn't even know the surgery was done. I had been under general anesthesia in a state of unconsciousness and a total lack of sensation.

When my parents told me it was all over I was so relieved, but at the same time felt extremely tired. I remembered that I had a surprise waiting and asked my parents what it was. They gave me a large stuffed animal; I think it was a fluffy white dog with floppy ears. I was really happy about my surprise then promptly fell asleep. I stayed in the hospital two more days and on the day I got to go home I had to learn how to walk with crutches before I could leave. I quickly learned and when my parents saw me whizzing down the hospital hall, they called me "Speedy Gonzales"!

The surgery was a success! While I was recovering that summer, I would often stare out at the lake daydreaming about all the sports I wanted to do, including speed water-ski racing like that girl I had seen the summer before. By the end of summer, my leg was all healed up, but it had been the longest summer ever, just sitting still while my leg was healing.

Post-surgery, I still had a smaller leg, because the doctors hadn't caught the problem when I was born. As a result, my leg was smaller in size and kids made fun of me. On my first day of school, it was awful! Mom bought me a beautiful red plaid dress for my kindergarten debut, but I came home crying because the kids had made fun of my leg.

That was the end of dresses for me. I was a tomboy after that. There was no way I was going to wear a dress to school after that first day.

My favorite TV show back then was "Batman," starring Adam West. I was hooked on this show and watched every episode. Halloween was around the corner and my mom took me to Gemco to get my costume. I was beside myself when I saw a Batman costume. I jumped for joy! I ignored all the other cute little-girl costumes. I was in Heaven! I thought I was a real hero and loved making believe that I was Batman. I ran around the house yelling the words to the TV show theme song: "Nah nah nah nah nah nah, Batman!"

I told my mom, "I'm gonna make a difference in this world, Mommy!"

I not only wore that costume for Halloween; I wore it for the next two years until my shirt ended up halfway up my stomach and my mom said it was too small. When we finally had to throw it away, I cried for days. I've never grown tired of Batman.

I made it through my kindergarten year counting the months to summer at the lake. In fact, every school year after that, all I could think about was my fun summers at the lake and all the excitement I knew was coming. We knew all our neighbors, and during the week we would get together about four or five boats, pack lunches, and venture around the lake, enjoying ourselves. It took the whole day to go around the entire lake. We would water-ski, swim, and go in these very smelly waters called the Soda Bay Hot Springs. The older folks would drink Cold Duck while I just played in the hot springs and climbed on the red rocks, getting my bathing suit completely dirty. After that was done, I would water-ski all the way home. I could hang on for the longest time. Sometimes I would ski through the green algae water and when I was done skiing my blonde eyebrows and blonde hair were pea green. I didn't care: I just wanted to ski.

One summer, the ducks got real sick so I made a sick bay for them in our large yard fronting the lake. I put up a fence and went up to the pharmacy to see what I could do for the ducks. I don't remember what the pharmacist gave me, but I do remember feeding the ducks some fluid with a dropper and it did help them. I saved many of the sick ducks.

We also had a small movie theater within walking distance of our lake house. I enjoyed going to the movies and getting two treats, popcorn with extra butter and M&M's. One of my favorite movies was *Herbie The Love Bug*. I thought our little movie theater was big, but actually it was very small. When you're a kid, everything seems big.

My best friend who lived across the street would get to ride in her dad's hot boat. It was called Blue Blazes, a hydroplane boat that could reach speeds up to 100 mph. It had the largest rooster tail and was really cool to watch. My dream was to one day be able to go for a ride in that boat. Dad never let me go, though, because he was worried about me going that fast in a boat. So one day, I snuck away and told my friend's dad that my dad said I could go. That was the thrill of a lifetime and I loved it, but boy oh boy did I get in big trouble when I got home. My dad had his binoculars and caught me flying by.

When I got home from my big ride, my parents confronted me and I felt bad that I disappointed them. They grounded me for the rest of the day and I disliked being in my room because I loved playing outside. I was a pretty easy kid to discipline and I usually learned my lesson after a day of being grounded.

When I was about seven, my dad installed a tetherball in the driveway. I played that game with all my friends. One day, the ball swung and hit me right in the mouth and chipped off my front tooth. It was something I took in stride because I was a big tomboy and drove my mom nuts with all my accidents. I was always skinning my knees or stepping on bees, because I liked being barefoot.

In grade school, I loved sports, playing kickball, baseball, and basketball. I really liked the fitness assessment testing the school did twice a year, which included the long jump and how many sit-ups and push-ups you could do in one minute. I was very competitive and ranked high on all the physical education tests.

The fun summers wound down to the Lake County Labor Day Fair. We lived close by so we could walk there. One of my favorite games to play was the dime toss. Dad would play the darts game and always win me one of those big stuffed toys. My favorite ride was the Tilt a Whirl. I also enjoyed seeing all the farm animals: horses, rabbits, goats, cows, and pigs. We ate corn dogs for dinner and on the way home from the fair we got fabulous cinnamon rolls. They were the best! To this day, I still go to the fair every year and love those cinnamon rolls, especially with extra frosting.

I got very sad when the summers would end, not only because they were so much fun, but because I had to go back to school. I dreaded school mainly because of how the kids would bully me about my smaller leg.

And then there was this one very horrific incident: When I was about nine, I got molested by three much older neighborhood boys. They were teenagers, around fourteen to seventeen years old. The boys coerced me into doing sexual things with them.

I don't remember a whole lot because it was a very traumatic time for me, but I do recall the boys threatening me if I ever told my parents. Trying to figure out what to do, I shared what happened with a friend and she told her mom, who then told my parents. Mom and Dad talked to me and were very consoling and made me feel loved. They were not mad at me but furious with the boys and reported it to the police. They really helped me through this extremely difficult experience. The boys got in trouble with their parents, and from then on they were not allowed to come down to my end of the street, and I wasn't allowed to go near their side of the street.

I had about half a dozen close friends that I hung out with around my Sunnyvale neighborhood. They were nice friends that didn't make fun of my limp and smaller leg. My gang would climb the street poles at night and luckily our parents never caught us or we would have been mincemeat. After school, we would play games like "Green Light, Red Light," "Hide n' Seek," and "Simon Says." We also would play marbles. We each had a collection of different-colored marbles with neat designs. The goal of the game was to roll your marble down the gutter through all the obstacles like leaves and rocks and hit the other person's marble. If you hit it then you would get to keep that marble.

One afternoon after school, I got in a fight with a boy because he was teasing me about my smaller leg. I punched him in the face and he reported me to the principal. I got in big trouble and had detention after school for a week. I think the boy was embarrassed that a girl socked him in the mouth. He never messed with me again.

I loved the holidays. My mom and dad made the holidays very enjoyable. Mom decorated the house for every holiday. We started the year off with a fun New Year's Eve party with family and friends, most of whom had kids I really liked. Then, in February, my birthday month, my parents always made that special. For years, they hired Koo Koo the Clown and I invited all my neighborhood friends. I got lots of presents and my mom had fun games for us to play and usually a cool, decorated cake.

Valentine's Day and Easter were fun, too, and in the summer we celebrated the 4th of July in the normal American sense and also because it was my mom's birthday. I thought my mom was so lucky to be born on the 4th of July because everyone celebrated her big day. We would take the boat out in the evening and park on the lake to watch the fireworks that were set up on a barge near Library Park. It was such a thrill to be right under the fireworks. The only thing I disliked was all the mosquitos buzzing around.

Halloween was especially fun because Mom got the scariest decorations and played spooky music. All the trick-or-treaters loved to come to our house. My favorite Halloween was when I dressed up as Batman. When I got done trick-or-treating, my parents and I would sit around the kitchen table and divvy up all my candy. Mom loved the Snickers and my dad loved the Reese's Pieces. I loved it all.

In November, we would go to Oakdale and stay at my Uncle Jack and Aunt Betty's pigeon farm for the Moore Thanksgiving get-together. There were at least twenty to thirty of us every time. The best part was when my cousins let me ride their minibike. I didn't get to ride it very long, but I thought that was the biggest thrill. My passion for dirt bikes started there and continued into my adult life. At Thanksgiving dinner, there were about ten different pies to choose from. Berry pie was my favorite, topped with vanilla ice cream. I loved being together with my family and seeing all my cousins, uncles and aunts and grandparents. I also got to ride my cousin Heather's horse a few times.

For Christmas, Mom decorated the inside of the house with all kinds of bright decorations. We often went to the mountains together and picked out a fresh Christmas tree. Decorating it was my favorite activity. Mom would let me pick out a new ornament every year. She served Christmas cookies and eggnog and we played Christmas music while we decorated the tree. On Christmas Eve, my mom and dad would take me for a drive and we would look at all the Christmas lights and try to find Santa. I was a lucky girl because I got presents on Christmas Eve and Christmas morning. That was the fun part about being the only child. I got spoiled with lots of presents.

My childhood was great overall, but I wasn't always a little angel. A few times I pissed off my parents pretty good. I was around four years old and fascinated with writing my first name. I loved dotting the "I" with a large circle. Well, I ended up getting a coin and carving "Lori" in my mom's new stereo. After I did it, I realized I would probably get in big trouble so I put one of Mom's knickknacks over it and hoped she wouldn't notice. She did, the next morning. She asked if I'd done that and I said, "I don't think so."

"Oh, I see, then a little mouse did it," she said.

I started crying and she sent me to my room. After a few minutes of listening to me cry, Mom came in and hugged me and said, "God love ya, it's okay. Did you learn a lesson?"

I told her I did and promised not to carve my name in her things anymore.

When I was about ten, I didn't like my babysitter and one day I locked her out of the house and put my radio in the window so I couldn't hear her yelling at me. She called my mom at work and she had to leave to come home to handle the situation. Once again, Mom was not very happy with me. But I've learned throughout my life that forgiveness and compassion are two elements of her being that I've always been so grateful for. I do recall one time when I tried her patience a bit too much:

When I was eleven years old, we had a German shepherd named Zelda who had puppies. One day, Mom asked me to clean out the garage because the puppies opened up a bag of charcoal briquettes that got mixed in with all the puppies' poop. I looked at the mess and had the "bright idea" to just hose out the garage. As I was hosing the briquettes and poop down the driveway, my mom came home early and caught me red-handed. Boy, was I in trouble. I was grounded for a couple of days.

Other than these relatively benign incidents, I was a pretty well-behaved kid and I had nice manners. My parents taught me well. I was always respectful of other people because they were that way. That attitude extended to everything around me. I loved all kinds of animals and loved to care for them. I had pet ducks and a dog named Pepi.

Being born with a smaller foot and leg and having kids make fun of me all the time was very hard. My family was always there for me and I had the most fun with them because they loved me unconditionally. We stayed active doing fun things together. I enjoyed going places with my mom and dad and would rather be with them than other kids because I didn't have to be on-guard with them. I wished I had a brother or sister, though, because being an only child got very lonely at times.

My parents included me in everything. We had family dinners together and talked about what was going on in the world, and they always asked about my day. We had really good communication between us. We watched TV together after dinner and my parents watched the news and kept up on current affairs. I grew up listening to the news and news talk shows on the radio on our drives up to the lake. The news to me was a good thing. It kept us updated on world events.

You might even call my childhood idyllic. My mom would sing with me in the car—all sorts of uplifting songs. I loved going for rides in our white convertible, singing and having fun mother/daughter time. Mom played music at home, too. Music made me happy and later when I had my own kids, I played music in the car and sang with them and they loved it just like I had.

My parents were very caring about others and the world in general, and I inherited this good quality and maintained it throughout my growing up. I really liked people but could never understand how some kids could be so cruel, and couldn't understand the intention behind the mean things they would say to me. I eventually learned that everyone wasn't like me, and not the same from one person to the next. I learned to choose nice friends and decided at a young age to not ever be cruel to people, because I hated how this felt to me and never wanted anyone else to feel like that.

All things pass, and so did my happy summer lake days. When I was eleven years old, my parents got divorced and I was crushed! I was surprised when I found out my parents were getting a divorce because to me they seemed so happy. I'm not really sure why they did get divorced and I was very unhappy about it. Goodbye to the summer living at the lake. I still would go up on the weekends, but it wasn't the same as living there all summer.

I really took my parents' divorce hard. Between the ages of eleven and thirteen, I struggled with both my parents' splitting up and schoolmates still making fun of my smaller leg. I became extremely introverted and shy. I had a hard time in school because of the kids making fun of me. I didn't like to go to school at all; in fact, I hated it. Although my parents' divorce was a dark event, my life as a kid was highly enjoyable because Mom and Dad had very good family values and there was a lot of love. I never doubted how much my parents cared for me. I wanted this for my own family when I grew up and got married. Family was always Number One for me, but when I finally had one of my own, things would eventually turn out quite different than I had intended as a child.

That was because I did something very dumb—I got into Scientology.

Chapter Two

My Teenage Introduction to Scientology

All good things, like all other things, come to an end. My parents' marriage and our happy family splintered apart before I reached high school, and when I was about twelve, both my parents remarried.

Mom married a man who was a Scientologist, which at the time seemed rather innocuous. My dad married a non-Scientologist whom he met through his work. My mom's new husband's name was Jerry. They had been high school sweethearts. She was working at a golf course pro shop and Jerry came in the shop and saw her. He swept her off her feet quickly and they got married a few months later.

Jerry introduced both my mom and me to Scientology. I joined Scientology in 1976 at the age of thirteen. If I had known then that if I, Lori Moore, ever chose to leave the mission and as a consequence would lose my children, my family, and friends that remained in Scientology, I never would have participated, no matter what my situation was. I didn't have the luxury of such hindsight, however, so I entered the doors of the Stevens Creek Mission all wide-eyed and naïve.

Mom had a physical reason for joining. She was suffering from a sore shoulder and was also depressed about her grandma whom she was caring for. She was very close to her grandmother and increasingly sad as she saw her health declining rapidly.

To get you to sign up, Scientology gives you a "Personality Test" that always ends up with the evaluator seeing something that is your "life ruin," and they tell you it can get worse but Scientology can handle it. It hasn't changed in decades. So what was mine? I was very introverted and withdrawn. I was still upset about my parents' divorce and missed Mom and Dad being together. School was challenging and I struggled with meeting new friends after I moved away from my first home.

Mom went down to the Scientology center first but she wanted to know why it was called a Church because it was in a big office. They said, "Scientology deals with the spirit and mind and that's why it's called a church.

"Scientology also helps people with their self-improvement."

She told them that she and her daughter were Lutheran and would that be a problem? They said, "That's fine, you can be Lutheran and do Scientology."

After Mom got all her questions answered and took a Personality Test, she signed up for the first class which was called the Communication Course. She told me about the class and shared her "wins" with me. She asked me if I would like to come down with her one night and see what it was all about.

I went down to the Stevens Creek Mission in Santa Clara, California, and took the Personality Test. I saw what were supposed to be my weaknesses and strengths displayed on a graph in front of my face. My two biggest weaknesses at that time were my parents' divorce and my smaller foot and leg, which added to my shyness and made me feel very withdrawn.

After I took the test, a staff member took me to a private room, closed the door, and reviewed my results. The graph showed my two weaknesses and the person said, in a very intense tone, "Scientology can fix that! How would you like to not be bothered by these weaknesses anymore?" I was asked, and now she had a big grin.

I was excited about what I heard because I had never shared these two problems with anyone other than my parents. I felt like I had hope and could get over being so shy, which would result in having more friends.

After the results of my personality test had been discussed in depth, the staff member introduced me to the registrar (the person who tells you about the services Scientology delivers). I was told what service was best to help me with my weaknesses. After I was "closed" for the Communication Course, my mother paid for the service. Before I could start it, I had to see the Scientology Introductory Lecture, which I got totally lost in. After the lecture, I was sent to the Course Supervisor in charge of the Communication class. I learned I could not just start; I had to agree to a schedule. The minimum allowed participation was three evenings a week, but more was preferred.

The supervisor tried to get me to commit to studying on the weekends but I refused. "I'm with my Dad every other weekend and we do fun family things together."

My father was not a Scientologist and they knew that, so I believe they thought they had better keep things cooled off with him and not pressure me to be away from him.

I liked the Communication Course and made some new friends. One part of the class I struggled with was an exercise called "bull-baiting." This was where you have a "twin," someone you're paired up with in the class. After you learn how to sit in front of your twin for a certain length of time with your eyes looking into their eyes comfortably, your twin and other classmates take turns sitting in front of you and say all kinds of things to make you flinch, laugh, cry, or get upset. Each time you blow it and do not just sit there comfortably with no reaction, you get a big "Flunk!"—that's the actual word the person "bull-baiting" you says.

I was only thirteen years old and some of these people were much older and were swearing at me and making me embarrassed with sexual jokes. I got through it somehow then I had to be the one to bull-bait my twin and I struggled with that. It was really hard for me to pretend to be mean. It was not in my nature to do so. I couldn't wait to get through that section of the course.

My dad and stepmom found out about my participation in Scientology when I shared with them what I was doing in my evening class. They did not want me to be involved. A few weeks later, after I had been in my Communication Course for a while, Dad showed me a *Time* magazine article about Scientology being a cult. He gave me the magazine to show my mom. I told her about it and her husband, Jerry, said we both had to immediately go in to see the Ethics Officer at the Scientology mission. This was an individual in charge of any familial personal problems that arise that are interfering, or seen to interfere, with your progress up the "Bridge to Total Freedom" that Hubbard called the Scientology chart of training and levels of awareness. L. Ron Hubbard is the man who invented Scientology and Dianetics.

We were told to bring in the *Time* magazine article and instructed not to read it. The Ethics Officer told us that many people in the world who are Suppressive, which is Scientology's term for those critical of the church, are people who want to destroy Scientology. He said reporters and the media were all suppressive. He added that *Time* was suppressive and the article was full of lies and it was intentionally meant to try to stop Scientology. He said the article would get us really confused and be bad for us to read. So, I never even got to read it.

He then went on to tell my mom and me that news magazines like *Time* were not good for us to read, and that also applied to watching the news and reading the newspaper. People in the media weren't to be trusted and they just wanted to cause chaos.

While the Ethics Officer was telling us all this, I felt uneasy. When I look back at this time now, I imagine I was thinking of how my family raised me with the news being on television almost every night and my parents always reading the paper.

When you are in Scientology, however, from the very beginning you are taught not to question things Scientology tells you. If you do question something, then you are shown an LRH Policy (an official policy paper written by L. Ron Hubbard), and that LRH is the "Source" for all the knowledge in his religion. Actually, the Source name was left fairly wide open as to its meaning. Many people, I would learn, thought Hubbard was like God, so we needed to believe everything he wrote or said.

I soon began hating being shown policies if I questioned something, so I kept my mouth shut most of the time. I also disliked studying LRH policies because they were hard for me to understand. I eventually concluded that the Ethics Officer was one of the main people in the organization, who was an expert in mind control due to the way policies were enforced with its members.

I absolutely couldn't stand having to go in to see the Ethics Officer because I would be told to read a Scientology policy about "Handle or Disconnect" anytime I was up against someone who had any objection to or criticism of Scientology. I was manipulated to "handle" my father to not show me articles critical of Scientology any longer, because it became clear I would never disconnect from my own dad.

I was coached on what was called a "Good roads, fair weather" handling when talking to my dad and stepmom. That meant I was only to discuss things *other than* Scientology with Dad and my stepmom. The Ethics Officer would pretend to be my dad or stepmom and we would role-play as he said things critical of Scientology. I then had to learn how to get them off the subject and talk about other things like the weather. I also had to practice telling my dad and stepmom how I loved Scientology and that it made me feel bad when they criticized it. The Ethics Officer also told me to tell them that I didn't criticize my stepmom's Catholic beliefs, so she should leave me alone about Scientology.

I hated doing this stuff. I wish I could have just been honest with my non-Scientology parents and told them that Scientology was manipulating me to say those things. I didn't feel comfortable and my gut instinct was to feel uncomfortable about it. Nevertheless, after I spent many days learning how to do this "Good roads, fair weather" handling, I used that with my dad and stepmom and just got used to feeling uncomfortable. In retrospect, I see what an awful way it was to go through life whenever I was around Dad and my stepmom. Each time I saw them I would hope they wouldn't bring up Scientology because I hated this pretend game I was brainwashed into playing.

This was my first wakeup call that there was something very, very wrong about Scientology, but I was a teenager and felt stuck in the situation because my mom and stepdad were also involved in the Hubbard religion. I knew I couldn't be critical of Scientology because if I was, then that Ethics Officer would try to make my mom disconnect from me. I knew my mom never would disconnect from me but I didn't want her and my stepfather to have any pressure or problems caused by me—so I just continued on with my classes.

When I first joined Scientology, though, I liked some of the things I got from it. I felt it enhanced my communication skills and improved my life.

After the Communication Course, I continued taking classes in the evening. The people at the mission said I would do better if I went to class five nights instead of just three, so I decided I had to do this because everyone else was, and I wanted my class supervisor to stop pressuring me. There went my two nights at home. I signed up for classes Monday through Friday. My friends at school would talk about all the fun things they did in the evening, particularly on Friday. Friday night dances? I would miss them, just as I would miss going to the movies with my friends. I felt isolated from my non-Scientology friends because all I was doing every weeknight was attending class at the mission.

When I turned fourteen in 1977, my stepdad got a job in San Diego so my mom and I moved with him to Solana Beach, a town in San Diego County. We got a condo at the Solana Beach Club. It was awesome there. I was within walking distance of the beach and this is where I learned how to surf. I attended Torrey Pines High School where I met a special boy the first week I arrived. We became boyfriend and girlfriend and he taught me to ride the waves. My stepdad was doing real estate and my mom got her certification in Nutrition and worked as a nutritional counselor.

My stepdad got Mom and me to join him at the nearby Adams Avenue Scientology Mission. I told my boyfriend about Scientology and invited him to come with me one night to check it out. He liked what he heard and we both took a class called the "Survival Rundown." My boyfriend was my twin so that made going to class every night more fun. In this class, we learned some introductory "auditing" (counseling) techniques. We reviewed the Communication class and took a more advanced Communication class. We also learned how to control others by doing exercises that we drilled on over and over.

The best part for me at the new Scientology place was being able to be there with my boyfriend. I hated it when the supervisor would separate us and make us twin with different students. That started happening more and more, but on the weekends my boyfriend and I had fun just being kids. We would go surfing, hang out on the beach, and watch movies at his house. We were going steady for about six months when I found out my mom and stepdad needed to move us back to San Jose because my stepdad's job had not worked out. It was a huge crush on my budding love life, but what could I do? I was devastated that I had to leave my boyfriend. I told my mom and stepdad that I wanted to stay in San Diego. I said I liked the mission more there. I didn't say it was because my boyfriend was there with me, but they knew. My tactics to stay in San Diego didn't work. We said our goodbyes and back to San Jose my family went. My boyfriend and I stayed in touch for a few months after I moved, but he dropped out of Scientology. I don't think his parents liked him taking those classes.

Mom opened up her own business in nearby Campbell and called it Dee's Diet Counseling. My stepdad got a job at ROLM Corporation. We moved to the east side of San Jose, not the best part of town. I attended Independence High School and I hated it there. I was one of the only white girls at the school. I had no friends, and everyone looked at me like I didn't belong there, probably because of my blonde hair. Most of the kids were Hispanic so my look and beach style of dress did not fit in at all. I desperately wanted to be back at my high school in San Diego with my surfer boyfriend, who was now fading out of my life. I was struggling in school and my grades were poor.

My mom, stepdad, and I enrolled again at the Stevens Creek Scientology Mission in San Jose. All my old friends were there and I met new ones. When I went back, they had me take another personality test. My results showed that I was still very introverted and that I was struggling in school with my subjects and in making friends. They suggested that I take the basic grammar course and then "The Basic Study Manual" class, in which I would learn the Scientology way to study; then they said I would excel in school.

I started on the grammar course and had a very difficult time with it. Scientology teaches you to never read past a word you don't understand and to look up that word, making sure you understand every definition that word might have. Plus, you need to look up the derivation of the word. Every time I looked up the derivation, there were more words that I didn't understand. It was like trying to unravel a rat's nest. So now I was not only struggling in high school, I was struggling in my Scientology class.

Life was no longer fun. I kept telling the Scientology people that my studying was not getting easier. They told me to find my "misunderstood" (the word they were certain I had gone past) and to keep going.

Luckily, at school I finally made a new friend. She was nice to me and we started hanging out. She was Hispanic and I was so happy she accepted me. I found out after a couple of weeks that she regularly cut school and that influenced me to cut with her. She hated school like I did. We hung out one day at the mall. She tried on some clothes at J.C. Penney department store and I was shocked to see her put her own clothes on over them and then walk out of the store. I was so afraid we would get busted, but she got away with it. She said I should try it.

I was so nervous, but I didn't want to show it, so I acted tough and went to Macy's and tried on clothes and put my clothes over those and just walked out. Inside, I was scared to death, but just went home, hid my stolen clothes in my closet, and then went to Scientology for class.

A week later, my friend and I cut school again and went to a different mall. We didn't get away with it this time. I was in the Macy's dressing room next to my friend and when we walked out, two officers were there and arrested us. I couldn't believe I was being arrested for stealing. All I could think about was how upset my parents were going to be with me. I was in the back of a cop car with my friend and I had to hold back the tears because I didn't want her to think I was a wimp. Inside, however, I was terrified.

We were taken to Juvenile Hall where they booked my friend and me. They put us in a private room and my friend told me not to say anything. I thought she must have been through this before. Then they separated us. I was now alone in a room and scared to death. I'd never been arrested before and had been a pretty good kid until this happened.

A few hours later, my stepdad came to get me and then brought me to the Scientology mission to see my mom. It was late and she was in her Scientology class. I had to wait until she had a break to see her—Scientology was very strict about their course schedules. I was so ashamed of my actions and did not want to tell her what had happened. When we talked, I finally told her and blamed my actions on the school I was going to, my struggle with studying my subjects, and I shared how unhappy I was with my life. I told her I was very sorry and promised never to steal again.

I didn't want Mom to make me tell my father. She said I needed to do that. That same evening, I had to go see the Ethics Officer because of the theft. I remember telling him that I hated my high school and I was getting bad grades because I was trying to apply my new Scientology study skills but I couldn't do it at my school. I told him I would get really behind because of trying to look up every word I didn't understand.

"You just have misunderstoods!" he exclaimed.

Then he said I could go to a Scientology school and they would really help me with my study problem. I got excited about that idea; at least he wasn't dwelling on my arrest. But then the Ethics Officer made me do a set of ethics improvement "conditions" because I was in a "lower condition," far below "Normal." I had to do a series of steps outlined by Hubbard to get accepted back into the group. I started on my "conditions" that evening. I worked my way up to Liability, which is where you make up the damage to the group, meaning my Scientology group. As I was doing these steps, I was recruited to work with the mission staff. They told me it would make me a better person. I thought to myself that since I had screwed up so bad, this was my chance to feel better about myself and also I would be helping mankind in a big way, devoting more time to helping spread Scientology into the world.

After the recruiters told me how much I would be helping and that my mom would be proud of me, I was feeling better about myself. I wanted Mom to be proud of me again. I knew I had really disappointed her. So, after two years of being involved in Scientology, at age fifteen I signed a five-year contract with the Church of Scientology Stevens Creek Mission as an employee on a part-time basis. Mom also joined the staff, but she only signed a two-and-a-half year contract. She was livid when she found out I had signed one for five years without discussing it with her first.

The staff recruiters, you see, had separated us on purpose. Scientology believes that we are spiritual beings and that kids can handle the same responsibility as an adult, so I made the decision without my mom, stepfather, or dad being present.

On a positive note, I very much liked being treated like an adult. The recruiter made me feel really important and said that making the decision to join staff for five years was the best thing I could ever do. I was helping to save the planet! I thought it was true. The next day I began doing administrative duties such as grading personality tests and getting promotional materials ready to be mailed out.

During this time in 1978, I quit my public high school and joined a Scientology school in Los Altos called Sunreach, which was located about an hour away from where I lived on the east side. I got a ride with Mom to her work in San Jose then took the public bus to school and the bus to the

Scientology mission after school. At first, I liked Sunreach, where I met some nice girlfriends, Sly and Jolie, and a boy named Karl, who liked sports like I did. He and I played baseball and Frisbee and hung out at a deli by the school and ate cream cheese bagels, the best I ever had. We became boyfriend and girlfriend soon after we met.

Sunreach was a small school but not the perfection I had been promised. After several months, I started struggling with history. I was very slow compared to my friends. I was still trying to apply the Scientology study skills I had learned and it was still rough for me. I would get frustrated because it would take me hours to read one or two pages. Looking up all the words and derivations and all the words that I didn't understand in the original word definitions was like Alice in Wonderland down the rabbit hole. I couldn't finish my assignments and was getting far behind.

Soon Karl and I broke up because I liked an older boy whom I met at QuikMart, a convenience store where he worked as a clerk, near the Scientology center. A girlfriend from Scientology had taken me to meet him. His name was Randy. I was fifteen-and-a-half and Randy was twenty-two. He also went to the same Scientology mission that I did. I had an immediate crush on him and thought he was really cute. I really liked that he was older. He asked me out one day when I went to say hi after school. I couldn't believe that he had asked me out, since he was a lot older. I was so excited.

We ended up going together for about three years. I even brought him up to the lake to meet my dad and stepmom. They were concerned because he was much older than I. I acted a lot older than my age, because being on staff in Scientology made me grow up fast. Randy was an avid Scientologist and he wanted to be on course even on the weekends. I didn't want to do that; I wanted to go to the lake and be with my family and have fun water-skiing and lying out in the sun.

One summer, when Randy and I were at the lake and he was in a bad mood, he told me that he needed to get up "the Bridge" faster to achieve every Scientologist's goal of being at the top in auditing and training.

I got mad at him and said, "Can't you just enjoy being here with me at the lake? We have a beautiful lake house to be at and a nice boat to go water-skiing behind. What's wrong with you? All you want to do is be on course!"

After I said that, he wasn't very happy with me and the weekend was awful. I started going back up to the lake on the weekends without him. He would occasionally go, but I knew he would rather be on course. Randy was also very tight with his money. One weekend at the lake, my parents asked if he could go to the store and pick up some chicken for dinner to barbecue.

Randy told me as we went to the store that he hoped they paid him back. I couldn't believe how stingy he was. Even when we went out on dates we went Dutch most of the time. He had no problem with spending his money for his Scientology services, though.

Dating Randy and going to Scientology got more difficult. On the weekend, I would try to get caught up on my history lesson, and one day he asked if he could help me with my studies. He tried to help me look up my misunderstood words, but that only made it worse for me. I felt stupid trying to study with him. He would make hurtful comments that made me feel very inadequate. He couldn't understand why I just couldn't apply my study training from Scientology and get quickly through my history.

I ended up feeling extremely stupid and thought I had to drop out of school because I felt I could never get through it. I told my mom that I would get my General Equivalent Degree and that I wanted to get a full-time job and be on Scientology staff in the evening and take my classes. She was okay with that, but wished I would stay in school. My dad felt the same as my mom did. I never told Randy or my parents that the real reason I dropped out of the Scientology school was because I felt stupid. I just couldn't study the way Scientology had trained me. I felt I would never graduate at the rate I was going.

At sixteen, I got a full-time job soldering phone circuit boards at an electronics company. Because I had been in Scientology from such a young age, I grew up fast and acted like I was twenty. I fit right in with my coworkers who were at least ten years older than I. In the evening, I took my Scientology classes and worked for Scientology late at night and on some weekends.

Around this time, at the age of sixteen, I was actively recruited to join the Sea Organization, otherwise known as "the S.O."—the highest-ranked group within Scientology. I knew of the Sea Organization in Los Angeles and Clearwater, Florida. To be on staff in the S.O. means that one has to sign a billion-year contract to dedicate one's many lives to serving Scientology. When I was approached to join, I had a sick feeling in the pit of my stomach. Something didn't feel right and my instincts told me to say no.

Also, I was told by one of my friends that people in the S.O. didn't get to see their family much. I was very much a family-oriented girl so I was not interested at all! I loved going to the lake and spending time with my family. There was no way I was going to give up being with them or being away from my family.

As they do, the Sea Org recruiters intimidated me. I felt very nervous around them. Luckily, I got out of the long recruiting cycle most people endured. I don't remember how I did it, but from then on when I saw that the

S.O. recruiters were in town recruiting at the mission, I would stay clear of the place. Those people scared me with their pseudo-Navy uniforms, and I felt uneasy around them. They showed up at the Scientology mission often. I was finally able to change my hours to late in the evening without anyone knowing the real reason, which was to avoid those recruiters.

I dated Randy off and on over the next couple of years, worked at the ROLM Corporation electronics firm, and was on staff and took Scientology classes. Randy and I broke up for good when I was nineteen. He was not much fun anymore, as all he wanted to do was Scientology services. I started hanging out more with my friends and taking them up to the lake on weekends. I dated a couple of Scientology boys I met taking classes there, but nothing real serious developed.

In my fourth year on staff, I witnessed many odd things. In 1982, David Miscavige, who would eventually take over Scientology, along with a few other high-ranking Scientology officials held a gathering of successful Mission Holders to reprimand some of them for doing things incorrectly. The meeting was held in San Francisco only an hour away from the mission I belonged to.

During the meeting, Kingsley Wimbush, the Mission Holder of my Scientology Center, was there and he was declared a "Suppressive Person." Because of this, he was no longer allowed to be our mission holder.

During that time, S.O. members known as the Finance Police and dressed in black uniforms would come in and take over a mission in a very militant fashion and it created a frightening atmosphere. I hated being there. These "missionaires" wanted us to be on course more and go to every event, because you were more likely to spend money on Scientology. Events were held on Saturdays and we were expected to go. I was instructed to help the full-time staff wash their cars and donate money. One evening, I was in the course room taking a Scientology class and our normal ten-minute break time came. A hat was passed around and everyone was asked to donate money before we could take a break.

The pressure to donate kept getting more intense. It seemed so crazy and I wanted to get out of there. It was during this time that I started questioning whether Scientology was making me happy. I felt stressed more than ever when I went to the mission. I had to keep my Monday to Friday evening course schedule and get my work done each day, but besides that, I got much less dedicated and started having fun again. I went up to the lake in the summer almost every weekend.

My family made things better for me when I got away from town. At the lake, I didn't have to worry about being asked to donate more money that I didn't have. (Meaning that if you had a credit card or a way to borrow money, they would be all over you to gain access to that.) When I was at Scientology, it was all about what was the next service you would take and what more can you do to help "clear the planet." (The big first goal of any Scientologist was to reach the mental and/or spiritual state of Clear, which was first mentioned in the book *Dianetics*. Clearing the planet meant getting a large majority of the population on Earth through that state.)

I was getting sick of the pressure. I had a couple of Scientology girlfriends, Malena and Kathy. We hung out on our dinner breaks and sometimes on weekends. Kathy and I weren't perfect Scientologists. We would get some boys to get us beer, since we were under age, at the liquor store near the Scientology mission. Then we would drive around in my Ford Pinto and park somewhere away from the mission and drink beer. I think we were so stressed that we just wanted a break from our adult responsibilities. Listening to Led Zeppelin and drinking a few beers was a great stress relief!

I stayed one more year at the mission, finally finishing my contract with the church. I knew I needed to finish up my five-year contract, because if I didn't I would have to pay back Scientology for every course and bit of counseling I had been awarded for being on staff. I routed off staff in good standing.

I decided I wanted something very different. Despite the troubles I'd had with study over the years, I wanted a very different life. I was going to go to college!

Chapter Three

My Higher Education

After fulfilling my Scientology staff contract, I went to college for six years. That came about because Mom had divorced Jerry and married my new stepfather, Val, who got me to see that I really needed to get a college education. I struggled in college due to the fact that I had not received a full high school education, but amazingly I persisted and received my B.A. Luckily, I found out real quick that applying Scientology study technology in the real world didn't work. I actually flunked out my first year of junior college trying to study the way I had learned in Scientology. I was twenty years old in 1983 and most of my friends in junior college were a couple of years younger. I was horribly embarrassed that I couldn't pass that first year. I did well in physical education classes, but despite encouragement from Val and Mom, I was ready to drop out because of the frustration from trying to apply Scientology study skills. I felt lost.

I shared my frustration with Dad and was honest about my poor grades. He got me a private tutor for the summer who taught me basic grammar and how to study and write papers in college. The following two years after being tutored, I got my A.A. and graduated with honors.

In my second year of junior college, I tried out for the men's golf team, since the school did not have a women's team. The day I went to the golf coach's office I felt a little nervous just because I was a girl and this was a men's team. I reminded myself that in middle school I had been on an all-boys golf team and did well keeping up with the boys. But then I thought, we were only kids back then and the guys on this team are grown men and can probably hit the ball pretty far. Still, growing up playing golf with my grandpa and my uncles made me a better golfer. I always played from the men's tees. In fact, I had never played golf from women's tees. After I introduced myself to the coach and explained how I grew up golfing with my grandpa and uncles and had been on the middle school boys golf team, he gave me a chance. I told him I was very consistent and averaged about a 230-yard drive.

I don't think he believed me. He said, "Let's meet at the practice range tomorrow when I'm coaching the team."

When I showed up the next day, he said, "The team just started practicing and we're working on all parts of the game. I would like to see your swing and see if you can chip and putt fairly well."

I was so excited that he was going to give me a chance to try out! I surprised the golf coach with my ability to hit the golf ball as far as some of the young men on the team. He welcomed me to the team, but said I needed to follow the men's rules. I had to play from the men's tees and I could not get any special exceptions because I was a girl.

Then he clearly stated, "There is no dating your fellow-team members!"

I did keep my word by not dating any of the men on the team, but I had a big crush on the golf pro who taught at the course where we practiced. He was quite a bit older than I, in his early thirties. I still liked older men, which is why the young men on the team didn't appeal to me. After a few months of hanging around the golf course, one day after my coach and fellow-teammates had left, the golf pro, Tom, asked me out. After a couple of dates with him, though, I realized he was all about his good looks and his personality was boring. From then on, I concentrated on golf and school.

One moment that was exciting on the men's golf team was when I was playing the Stanford Golf Course in Palo Alto, California. I was tied with a guy on the opposing team. We were heading toward the 18th green. Both of us had landed our second shots on the green of a 430-yard Par 4 hole. I had a long putt and sunk it, making a birdie. My opponent missed his short putt and got par on the hole. I won by one point. I was so excited but as I looked over at my opponent he looked like he was crying. I thought maybe he never had a girl beat him in golf before. That made my day, and my coach was pretty happy with me. We ended up beating the team overall.

Golf was one of my passions and being able to play the sport every day was invigorating. My last year on the team, my coach said he was going to transfer to San Jose State and mentioned that the school had a women's golf team. He said I would do great on that team, but I told him I didn't know how to play from the ladies' tees! He laughed. I almost transferred to San Jose State, but my insecurities got the best of me. I've often wondered if I had taken that opportunity if I would have kept going and gone for the pro circuit. I wish I would have at least tried. Unfortunately, there was more Scientology ahead.

After I graduated from junior college, I checked out a few four-year colleges. Since I still lived in San Jose, though, I would get bugged to come down to Scientology and take classes or go to one of their Friday night graduations and hear people's wins from course. Somehow, I managed to keep my distance. If I didn't answer my phone when Scientology called, then I didn't need to get into a conversation explaining why I could not go down there. Avoidance was working for me. I was going to school full-time and working as a waitress at Bob's Big Boy about thirty hours a week. I was very busy and had barely enough time to study for school. This was a great excuse to not have time to go down to Scientology.

I was really liking my life. I felt somewhat normal and was enjoying school and working outside of Scientology. I made lots of new friends and realized people on the outside of Scientology were very nice. I decided I didn't want to join another golf team because I would have to be on the women's golf team and play from the women's tees, and that worried me. I didn't feel I could judge distance accurately from those tees.

Nevertheless, I checked out San Luis Obispo and a few other schools. My girlfriend Lisa, a good friend from junior college, told me about Chico State. We planned a trip there and both really liked it. I was twenty-three at that time, so I felt too old to be in a dorm. Lisa and I got our own two-bedroom apartment about a mile from the campus. My dad and her dad moved us in. We loved our little apartment. I was off to the big university!

I loved going to school at Chico State. I was having fun being a college student and being away from Scientology. It was during this period that I learned that L. Ron Hubbard had died. I was surprised to hear that and wondered what would happen with Scientology with Hubbard gone. Also, during this time, I wasn't being pressured to come back to Scientology and take classes because I was so far away.

I met lots of neat friends and realized again that they didn't have to be Scientologists to be good people. You see, Scientology labels people that are not Scientologists "wogs"—a term from when Britain ruled India. It's an acronym for Worthy Oriental Gentleman, a derogatory term to the Brits. I always hated that *wog* label. In Scientology, we were taught that Non-Scientologists are Middle Class and not as able as Scientologists. I never believed that, though. In fact, I found all these new people in my life to be very pleasant and easy to talk to. I dated a few boys my first year at Chico State, then I fell head-over-heels with an older man.

Unfortunately, he was married. He was much older, and I think that is what attracted me most. Since he was married, I tried to like other boys, but I couldn't get over the strong infatuation I had with this man. The boys at Chico were younger than I was and seemed very immature. My second year there, this older man, Rick, and I became good friends and he shared with me that he was not happy with his wife and that he was going to leave her. I thought there was hope for us and that one day soon we could be together.

He said things to me like, "You're the best thing that has happened to me. You're beautiful and the one I want to be with."

I naïvely believed him. He promised that he was going to get divorced so he could be with me. I was gullible and fell for his lies. He came over to my apartment and we slept together. I thought I was so in love with him and couldn't believe that we actually made love. When he left in the middle of the night he said to me, "It was wonderful being with you. I'll see you soon."

I asked him when I would see him next. He said he had plans with a friend the next day and was going to a car show near the campus. I hoped he would invite me, but he didn't. He told me that he would call the following evening. After he left, I felt worried and uneasy. I woke my roommate up and told her what happened. She was concerned and was worried about me. I asked her if she would go to the car show with me because I wanted to run into him; I just couldn't go a day without seeing him.

My roommate agreed to go with me the following day, a Saturday when I had no classes. I got up early because I couldn't go back to sleep after he left. Later, when we got to the car show, I drove around until I found Rick's car. Since he was already there, we parked and got our tickets. As we went in the front gate, I spotted him. He was holding hands with his wife and laughing and having fun. He saw me and turned white. I walked up to him and said hi, but I kept my cool and walked away.

I left with my roommate as soon as we could find the exit. I stayed in my car after I drove her home and cried for hours. This man that I was in love with had broken my heart more than anyone ever had. He had lied to me just to get me in bed. He said he wasn't happy with his wife and was going to leave her for me. What a lie! I was devastated. I couldn't sleep or eat. I skipped classes the whole next week and got very depressed. I felt betrayed and used. It was awful! I called my mom and shared what had happened. I told her I didn't know what to do to help me feel better. She was really worried about me.

My mom was still doing a little Scientology so she told a Scientologist friend what had happened and he said he could help me. He was a Scientology auditor (counselor) in a Field Group, which is different than a Scientology Mission. Field groups were like subgroups outside of larger Scientology organizations.

I liked this idea of talking things over with this guy because I wouldn't have to go to a mission or an "org" (Scientology organization) and it felt less restrictive. I wouldn't have to worry about dodging those Sea Org recruiters that hung out at the missions and orgs. Mom said I wouldn't be pressured like I had been at the mission and I could set my own schedule. I talked with the counselor on the phone and agreed to go to San Jose the next weekend to meet him. I decided that I desperately needed help because of what had just happened and agreed to get some auditing with him. I would go to Chico during the week for my classes and come back to San Jose on the weekends to get auditing.

When I received the auditing, I did feel better and started forgiving myself for making that huge mistake of having an affair with a married man. My counselor had me do "ethics conditions" after my auditing session so I could see what I did to "pull in" all the emotional pain I'd suffered. I decided it was my "out-ethics" (not living in an ethical way) that made me pull in this married man and let him hurt me.

I finished up my actions with the field group auditor and was back trying hard to focus on my studies, although I still felt bad over Rick and had a hard time keeping my mind off him. Despite our interaction, I thought I was still in love with him. I was on the rebound for a long time and tried to date guys but always thought of the man who broke my heart. I believed that as a result of having to grow up so fast when I was a teenager on staff at Scientology, it made it difficult for me to date boys my own age and maybe that was why I tended to fall for older men.

My last year at Chico State, and shortly after my counseling with the field auditor, my girlfriend Mari introduced me to one of her friends. Mari was a Scientologist and so was her friend. I agreed to meet him so he set up a time when I was home for the weekend and I went over to her house for dinner. It would be like a double date. She told me ahead of time that he was five years older than I and that he was cute. His name was Jim Leake. I remember driving over to her house thinking I wasn't ready yet, as I was still stuck on Rick. I almost cancelled, but I didn't want to disappoint my friend after she went out of her way to cook a nice dinner for the four of us.

When I met Jim, I thought he was cute and nice. We had a nice conversation over dinner. Then, shortly after dinner, he asked me to go to Lyon's

Coffee Shop to have coffee. While we were there, he began going over the Non-Existence Formula with me, which is one of the Scientology "conditions" that you do when starting out with someone new, or working at a new job, or living in a new town, and you want to get to know people.

Jim was a lot higher up in Scientology than I was. He'd done a lot more training and auditing, and I felt a little nervous about that. I reasoned—back in a Scientology way of thinking—that with all his training and my previous lack of good judgment with relationships, I should hear what he had to say and take a look at this condition he was presenting. I learned he used to be a course supervisor at Scientology in the evenings. I was so happy he was not still supervising in the evenings, because he would have time to be with me if we dated. Before we looked at the condition as a method of starting some kind of relationship, though, I told him that I had a difficult time with studying Scientology nomenclature. He said he could help me with that. He was very understanding and I felt he really "duplicated" me, Scientologese for "perfectly understood my communication."

So I looked at this Non-Existent condition and got lost right away. Supposedly, all "conditions" had a formula which when followed step by step got you to the next, higher condition. Jim explained to me that if two people were thinking about having a relationship, the Non-Existence Formula was very useful to help them both see if the other person could really do what was needed and wanted by his or her potential partner.

I agreed to do this condition with Jim that night. Remember, this was our first date. It seemed awfully fast to be doing this kind of thing, but I agreed. As we did each step, we seemed to be a good match for each other, although I compromised on a few big things that bothered me. Jim told me about his finances. He was going through a bankruptcy, but he was doing payments and getting the situation handled, he said. He also told me that he owed the IRS money and was working on handling that, too. The thing that worried me the most, however, was that he was higher in Scientology than I was, and I was worried he would spend all his time on that. He said he liked to do other things, too, like hiking and hunting and going to the beach.

After we completed the steps of this condition, we decided to commit to having a relationship. After our date, I was driving home and felt like I had really rushed this thing. I knew I was still on the rebound but was hoping that diving into a new relationship would help me get over Rick.

I dated Jim for a couple of months then he moved in with me at my Chico apartment so I could finish up school. I graduated from Chico State with a B.A. in Physical Education and a minor in Nutrition. It had taken me three years, as I still struggled a bit. Before I had met Jim, I was planning to stay at Chico State and get my teaching credentials, but that would take another year. We wanted to get married. Jim proposed to me during my last semester. I said yes, but still had feelings for Rick.

I remember at one point we called off the engagement. I told Jim that I felt I wasn't ready for marriage and that it really bothered me that we were the same height. I also didn't like it that my hands were slightly bigger. I knew this probably hurt him, but I had to be honest. I let Jim convince me that I should not be into bodies so much and that those things should not be the deciding factor on whether to marry him or not.

Jim was very manipulating and used his higher status in Scientology against me, always with the attitude that he knew more than I did and that I should listen to him. I compromised and felt bad I had told him those negative things and I went along with the engagement. I did share with my dad that at one point I was going to call off the engagement, but that I had decided to go through with it.

Dad warned me that I might be making an unwise decision to marry Jim because of his bad financial condition. I should have listened. Dad was right! I never got my teaching credentials. Jim and I moved back to San Jose and instead of being a Physical Education teacher I went to work for my mom as a nutritional diet counselor. My grandma worked at Dee's Diet Counseling, too.

I really liked working at Dee's and being with my mom and grandma, but being back in San Jose put me in jeopardy. It would lead to my being drawn back into Scientology in a deep and eventually dangerous way.

Chapter Four

A Scientology Marriage, and Children

I married Jim Leake on December 21, 1988, thus becoming Lori Leake. Jim wanted to have a Scientology ceremony and I agreed. We had a beautiful evening wedding at our friends John and Frankie's home in San Jose with about seventy-five guests. After our wedding and reception, Jim and I stayed at the Fairmont Hotel in downtown San Jose. I remember sitting alone in the bathroom of our room holding back my tears while thinking to myself that I had made a huge mistake marrying Jim. I knew I was on the rebound and still had feelings for Rick. Crazy, I know, but I felt stuck and couldn't disappoint my parents after they had spent close to eight thousand dollars on our wedding.

I pulled myself together and joined my husband in our first night of marriage. We didn't have much money for a nice honeymoon, so after our one night at the Fairmont we ended up staying at the home of the people who hosted our wedding. We agreed to house-sit and watch their daughter while they went out of town for a couple of weeks. As soon as that was arranged, Jim announced he had decided to help out at the Scientology mission where I had been on staff. He told me he was going to be supervising every night during the two weeks when we were housesitting. This was right after our wedding day. I got very upset with him and told him I didn't want him to do that.

"Don't you want to be with me in the evening?" I asked.

He said that he needed to do it. I couldn't understand why he didn't just say no. I was upset with him for a while after that, and I regretted that I had married him. I was starting to see how committed he was to Scientology and how I was still not that committed. I was again in what Scientologists would call a "condition of Doubt" about Jim.

Somehow, I managed to get over my being upset with him. We found a house to rent near my dad's house on Alum Rock Avenue, a two-bedroom close to Alum Rock Park. Dad and I would run in the park a few mornings a week. I enjoyed spending one-on-one time with my father.

During the first couple of weeks in our new home, Jim and I got in another big fight. It bothered me that he would talk to his ex-wife on the phone while I was there. They would talk and laugh. I told Jim it upset me. He told me to stop being jealous. Then he said he was going to have lunch with her. I got really angry and told him I couldn't handle that and we got in a huge fight. I was so upset I was thinking of telling Jim I didn't want to be with him anymore. Our marriage was not going well. I was not very happy with him, but felt I needed to give it more time.

Our sex life was also not that great. I had actually never really enjoyed sex with any man. I always felt inadequate, shy, and introverted when having sex. I'm sure those feelings were coming from when I was molested as a young girl. I remembered reading romantic love stories during summers at the lake when I was about sixteen. I always used to imagine finding my Prince Charming like in those romance novels and having a happy ending. This marriage with Jim, however, was not how I imagined my life would be. It was nothing like I read about in my novels or envisioned. I told Jim that I wanted our marriage to be romantic like I pictured it to be when I read those novels. He told me that those were not reality and if I really wanted that then I should create it. So, since I was married to him, I tried creating that with Jim, but I just couldn't do it. You can't make something into reality that really isn't there to be made.

During our first year of marriage, Jim got an offer to work for a Scientology field group that delivered basic courses and counseling. Jim's job would be based in Chicago, Illinois. He was told that he was going to make about $60,000 a year being a Supervisor working for that field group. The problem was, I was very happy working for my mom as a nutritionist; something I went to school to learn. I also loved being around my family. I was very hesitant about making this big move and leaving my family and job. Jim painted a nice picture, telling me we could get a farmhouse and live in the country. We could make it there, he said. The San Francisco Bay Area was too expensive and we would never own our own home if we stayed where we were living. This was our big chance and we could have our dream home in the country.

Once again, Scientology overruled my judgment. My mom got me free auditing with a student who was on his internship to become a certified auditor. I was doing my "Grades" with him. These were Scientology auditing levels designed to help you with communication problems and other areas of trouble in your life. I was winning with my auditing in addition to being happy with my job. On the other hand, Jim and I were struggling to pay our bills, so having any extra money for Scientology counseling was not an option. I was a lucky girl to be able to get the Grades counseling for free. I babysat my counselor's kids in exchange for his auditing, but that was my entire cost. Scientology's teachings taught us to always have exchange "in" (equal value traded) with another person who does something for you. Jim said that the field group that he was going to work for would continue my auditing for free, because Jim would be working there. Naïve once again, I believed all the bullshit Jim was telling me. I would learn too late that the field group promised us all these things just to get us there.

After much back and forth, we packed up and moved to Chicago. I was really sad to leave my great job with my mom and grandma, as well as saying goodbye to all my friends, my dad, and family. Mom was very upset and she tried to talk me into staying. But Jim had me convinced that things would be better there and I felt I needed to stand by my husband. I wish I had listened to my mom. She knew this was a bad decision.

During the seven months I was in the Chicago area, we ended up in big financial trouble. The $60,000 that my husband was told he would make never happened and we were living in an apartment, not the country dream house my husband had described to get me to move to Illinois. Jim still had the required payments to make on his bankruptcy settlement that he had before we got married. Creditors were calling me during the day asking for their monthly payments. Other creditors were calling for past due payments. We were so broke we could barely pay rent, let alone have much money for food. Jim kept telling me that it was going to take some time until he started making more money. I was so stressed out both due to our finances and missing my family and friends back in California.

Before long, I decided that I couldn't continue to do this. I called my dad and mom and said I was probably going to come home; that I was very unhappy. Both my parents were happy to hear that news. It was about this time, however, that I found out I was pregnant with our daughter Jessica. I decided to give my marriage another go. I told myself that I had to find a way to make our marriage work for her. I knew how hard it was on me when my parents got divorced and I didn't want my daughter to go through that. I was also trying to figure out if I should go back to school to get my teaching credentials in Illinois, or stick with trying to find a job as a nutritionist. I still missed working for my mom and felt really lost.

I did go down to my husband's work and got an auditing session from one of the auditors in the field group. His name was Bill. I didn't feel comfortable talking to him, which made the counseling difficult for me. I noticed it was different than the kind of auditing I had had before. He asked me questions that were uncomfortable to answer. I didn't know what I was going to do about it. I didn't want to tell Jim or Bill that I didn't like being in Illinois and that I didn't like my new auditor. I had no one to talk to, so I just kept my thoughts to myself.

I was also nauseous with my pregnancy. It didn't help that I was taking a class at the Chicago Scientology Organization called the Student Hat Course. Wouldn't you know, it was a course to help one learn to study. We lived in Elgin, Illinois, about an hour's train ride from Chicago. I would take the train since we only had one vehicle. Jim would drive our truck into the city for work and I didn't want to be stuck there all day and evening waiting around for him. Jim worked six days a week; he left at eight in the morning and got home around ten-thirty at night. Sometimes we had Sundays together.

I hated taking the train because I didn't feel very safe traveling alone to and from the big city. This was in the winter, January 1990. I had heard people talk about how the El train in Chicago was dangerous, so I was nervous every time I rode it into the city. It went through some pretty bad parts of Chicago and made lots of stops to pick people up and drop them off. I felt like I was in another world and it made me even more homesick.

I had to walk about half a block after I got off the train to the Chicago "org." I felt uneasy going back to Scientology. On the first day, they wanted me to set up my course schedule. I hated that. It reminded me of when I was a teenager and had to have a schedule for my course time. But I went ahead, met my supervisor, and got my twenty hours-a-week part-time schedule. I was able to get out of a full-time schedule because I was pregnant and had morning sickness 24/7, plus I had the long commute.

The course room had about six to eight other students during the day. I was there from ten a.m. to five p.m. I had lunch by myself most of the time. I walked across the street to a coffee shop to avoid being approached by any staff members or Sea Org recruiters at lunch. I had a hard time feeling comfortable at this org and making friends. I struggled on my study course, too. I was not liking the Chicago situation at all.

After about a month on the study course, on one of my lunch breaks, I had another encounter with a Sea Org recruiter. This time, I had the best excuse in the world.

Bearing children while in the Sea Organization is forbidden. Nevertheless, during my pregnancy with Jessica, I was approached once again to join the S.O. I told the recruiter that my husband, Jim, was not qualified for the S.O. and the recruiter said that joining the S.O. was for the "greatest good" and not to worry about my husband. This she said to me, a married pregnant woman.

I looked at her with disgust and thought to myself, *you can take your greatest good crap and shove it!* After that happened, I didn't go back. I didn't tell Jim that I got pressured to join the Sea Org because I knew I would get reprimanded and sent to Ethics if I said anything critical about the mighty Sea Organization. I just said that I was too sick with my morning sickness to be on course. I also told him that I didn't feel safe taking the train into the city by myself. Thank God, I got off that course and the stressful schedule. I knew the stress wasn't good for me or my baby.

Another thing that happened when we lived in Illinois was that Jim invited his three half-brothers to a Scientology event and he wanted me to go, too. I hated these events because they always pressured us to donate money and I was afraid the Sea Org recruiters would be there. Still, I felt I had to go just to keep up good public relations and make my husband happy. So off I went with Jim, his mom, and his three half-brothers—Johnny, Billy, and Bobby. Billy and Bobby were twins.

My worry about the Sea Org recruiters was legitimate. They were there and the event was all about joining the Sea Org. Scientology put on a big presentation with elaborate details and fancy food. Jim's brothers all got recruited and signed up, signing a billion-year contract to dedicate their many lives to working for Scientology. I think they recruited my husband, too, but as I had told them before he was not eligible to join. (There were a number of reasons that disqualified a person, such as having taken LSD.) I was able to dodge talking to the recruiters by hanging out in the bathroom for a long time. I think they even tried to recruit Jim's mom. She didn't join, but she did start doing Scientology after that. A few days later, we said goodbye to Jim's brothers.

The creditors continued to call almost daily and now the IRS wanted payments from Jim's years of back taxes owed. They were going to garnish his wages and he barely made any money. I couldn't stand the pressure of our finances. I went out one day and applied for jobs at grocery stores. I didn't let them know I was pregnant. I got a job at Eagle grocery store in Elgin, a few blocks from our apartment. I knew that extra money would help a lot. They hired me as a checker and I was happy to have found a job so quickly. I told them that my husband worked in the city six days a week so I was available any time. I worked about thirty hours a week, battling daily morning sickness without letting anyone at work know. I made some nice friends at the store.

I had to learn how to drive in the snow real quick, though, and that was also challenging. Jim had to show me how to put our Toyota pickup in four-wheel drive. That was not an easy thing to do. The four-wheel trucks built in the 1980s were difficult to shift. One evening while going home late in a snowstorm, I slid off the road and that scared the crap out of me. Luckily, I only went into a ditch, dinging up our truck slightly.

I worked at the grocery store for four or five months. It was June 1990 and my mom was planning a baby shower for me back home in California. I was counting the days. Mom paid for my flight to help us out. The day finally came that I got on that flight back to California. I managed to arrange a week off work. I was seven months pregnant and still no one knew at work.

When I got off the plane and saw my mom, I hugged and hugged her and never wanted to let her go. She had a bouquet of balloons for me. She said I looked a little skinny for being seven months pregnant. We got my bags and went to a quaint little coffee shop in downtown Campbell. Mom knew me too well and could see I was holding things back. She asked me, "How are you *really* doing?"

I started bawling and couldn't stop. I told her I hated my life. I couldn't stand the pressure of the creditors calling us all the time. I said Jim was not even making enough money to pay our bills. We struggled with having grocery money and it was hard working at the store because I felt sick all the time. I told her that we argued a lot and I didn't know what to do. I shared what happened with the field auditor and what happened when I was at the Chicago org. I told her I knew my unhappiness was not good for the baby. She made me feel a lot better and kept what I had shared between us. Just having my mom to be with and talk to made a world of difference. I felt much better.

My baby shower was scheduled for Saturday and it was already Thursday, so we had one day to get ready. I had a wonderful shower and got to see all my family and friends. I was supposed to fly back to Illinois on the following Monday. I woke up on Sunday and told my mom I didn't want to go back. I hated it there and was really homesick. My life in Illinois was nothing like Jim had promised. Mom said if I didn't want to go back I could stay with her and have the baby in California so I wouldn't be under so much stress. I loved that idea, but was scared and worried about telling Jim. I finally got up the confidence to call my husband and share how I felt and say that I couldn't come back. I asked if he could please come back to San Jose and if we could move back home. I told him that my mom offered for us to live with her until we got back on our feet.

Jim didn't want to move back. I then said I was staying, anyway, because I couldn't go back to that life. I was too stressed out and worried about our baby. After hours of talking, we came up with a plan. I stayed with my mom and Jim gave his notice at the field group. He packed up all our stuff and returned to California. We moved in with my mom that summer.

On August 25, 1990, I had my beautiful daughter Jessica. She was a gorgeous baby. Jim and I were both happy to have our sweet baby girl. When I would take her out to run errands, people would stop and say, "You have a beautiful baby girl. She is breathtaking!" I loved her more than anything.

Jim was doing handyman jobs while studying for his contractor's license. I got a job at Lucky's Grocery when Jessica was around three to four months old. I learned that if I worked at least twenty-four hours a week I could get health insurance for my family. Jim and I debated over that. He didn't think we needed health insurance, but I did, and I had found a job that offered it. I knew several Scientologists that didn't have health insurance. Maybe that was the norm for them, but not for me.

I worked there for a year and we continued to live with my mom and stepdad. I didn't get very many weekends off, but when I did I wanted to go to the lake. Jessica started going to the lake when she was a baby, just like I had done. I wanted my kids to grow up with that wonderful lake life, too. Jessica loved to go boating in her Papa's (my dad's) boat. I would hold her in my arms and the sound of the boat engine would always put her to sleep. When Jessica was one year old, she went to the Lakeport County Fair like I had done at one year. I pushed her all around the fair in her stroller and she loved all the animals. Her favorites were the horses and rabbits.

After a year of living with my mom and stepdad, Jim and I got another side job managing an apartment building in Los Gatos. We got free rent with the condition that we took care of all the maintenance and cleaning of the other units when they came up for rent or needed repairs. I still worked at the grocery store and Jim kept doing construction.

My stepdad, Val, was an attorney and he advised Jim on our finances, suggesting he take care of his IRS bill immediately. It was $60,000 and they were ruthless and hounding him with penalties. We had no savings and didn't know what to do. Jim had gotten an IRS bill because he did not take taxes out for a couple of years for a job he worked at before I met him. Instead, he spent most of his money on Scientology and neglected other financial responsibilities.

My stepdad helped us do an offer of compromise with the IRS. They settled for six thousand dollars with the agreement that we stayed current with our taxes for the next several years. If we didn't stay current, then the $60,000 debt would be back in force. I explained the situation to my dad and asked him if we could borrow the six thousand dollars to pay the IRS and then make payments to my dad and stepmom. Dad was angry that I didn't listen to him before I married Jim but he did end up helping us. Since I was now married to Jim and the IRS debt was not taken care of before we were married, I was now a responsible party. After that, I made sure our taxes were paid each year no matter what, and it was stressful, to say the least.

I was very unhappily married. I wasn't in love with Jim. We didn't have much fun together. We were always stressed over finances. I still wanted to try to make our marriage work for our daughter. I told Jim that I wasn't happy, but that didn't help much. One day at the grocery store, I opened up to a fellow-employee. He was older than I. I ended up sharing with him how I was unhappy in my marriage and that I didn't know what to do. He was unhappy in his marriage, too. Well, that is what he told me. I was still gullible. We ended up having an intimate encounter because I felt intimidated. We were talking in his truck after work in the parking lot. He pressured me into pleasuring him and fortunately I was able to summon up some courage and got out of his truck quickly before anything else happened. I told him, "I can't do this and I need to get home." I also made up that I saw someone looking our way in the parking lot, which probably worried him.

This situation seemed eerily similar to when I was a young girl and how the boys had said things to get me to do sexual things to them. I don't remember what this older guy said to me, but I do know I was scared, I felt really bad afterward, and was very upset at myself, so that clearly told me the situation was not solely my idea and sex was not something I wanted to do with him. I went home and told Jim what happened, but left out the part that the guy manipulated me. I sat in my car before going in the house and thought it was best for my whole family not to tell Jim that the guy strongly influenced me in this action.

In Scientology, we are taught to not have a "withhold," which is something that one does and does not want another person to know. According to Hubbard, it follows an "overt," which is defined as a harmful act. I couldn't keep this withhold from my husband so I told him about the gist of the situation. I also told Jim that I was miserable with our marriage and that is why I did what I did. I didn't share the whole truth and that the guy manipulated me, because I knew Jim had a temper and I didn't want him to go after the guy and hurt him and then be in trouble with the law. Scientology had trained me to always take responsibility for my actions, so that is why I left out the part about the guy manipulating me. I should have known better not to get in that man's car to talk to him.

When I started Scientology, I always took responsibility for things that happened. If a Scientologist got sick or had something bad happen it was always the sick person that "pulled in" the bad action, or the Scientologist was connected to a Suppressive Person and was affected (weakened), becoming what Hubbard called a Potential Trouble Source (PTS). Jim didn't mention anything to me about my having "pulled in" this to happen when I was telling him about it. He got really upset and went over to the man's house the next day, threatening him that he'd better stay away from me. I can't imagine what would have happened if I had told Jim that the guy also manipulated me. What would he have done?

Jim took me to Scientology to see the Ethics Officer. We went together and the conclusion was that both of us needed to do the "Marriage 2-D co-audit," which was an action for partners in a "second dynamic" relationship who were having problems with each other. In Scientology, there is the belief that there are eight urges in life and the second one has to do with sex and procreation.

We had no extra money to do this Scientology action. I was trying to figure a way to pay for it, since it was my "out-ethics" (moral transgression) that got us to this point. In the meantime, I had to do the Scientology ethics conditions to make up the damage to my husband. I had fallen into the bottom condition of Treason by getting involved with the other man. I did every condition from the bottom up and did hours of amends to Jim for what I had done. I felt like I was an awful person for doing this and hated myself for it. I still was not happy in my marriage. Jim told his half-brother, Bob Wright, who was now in the Sea Org, what had happened and how we had no money to do this 2-D co-audit. Bob got his wife's mother, Minty Alexandra, who was a top auditor in the Sea Org, to deliver the action to us for free, since we were family.

Problem was, we had to figure out how to get to Clearwater, Florida, to do this at the Flag Service Organization—the main Scientology establishment. Jim and I worked out the flight costs and a place to stay. We flew to Illinois first to drop off our daughter with Jim's mom, and then we flew to Florida to do the 2-D co-audit. I was not very excited about doing this, because I honestly did not want to stay married to Jim, but I was trying to see if this action would help me feel better about my marriage.

We were on the 2-D co-audit for over two weeks. In this counseling, Jim and I were both in the room with Minty, the auditor. We took turns answering her repetitive question, "Lori, what have you done to Jim?" Then after I answered, the next question was, "Lori, what have you withheld from Jim?" This went on for a while, the same questions asked over and over then Minty switched to my husband. It was, "Jim, what have you done to Lori?" He answered and then she asked, "Jim, what have you withheld from Lori?"

Two weeks of grinding on this every day and we still were not done! We had to leave. I could only get two weeks off work and I didn't want to lose my job. When we left for Illinois to pick up our daughter, I wanted to try again with our marriage, at least for Jessica. I didn't want her to have divorced parents. Jim and I had made up at least a little. While we were in Illinois, I got pregnant with my son Jeremy. I realized this six weeks after we got back home. I started feeling nauseous again and knew I was pregnant.

I tried to be positive and had high hopes my marriage would get better. I was thankful I still had my job at the grocery store because I had insurance for our family. The fellow-employee I'd gotten wrapped up in emotionally transferred to another store, thank God. I never wanted to run into him again. Our financial situation, however, did not improve. We were continually struggling with bills and couldn't make it financially, so we quit managing the apartments and moved back in with my mom and stepdad.

I stayed home dealing with my contractions with Jeremy as long as I could. Jim and my mom drove me to the hospital and we barely made it in time. We got there at six a.m. and Jeremy was delivered at six-thirty on June 9, 1993. He was perfect, just like Jessica. He was a big baby at 9.6 pounds and I had him naturally. Jessica had been a big baby, too, at 8.75 pounds. Her birth had taken longer, over twenty hours, and I had taken Demerol for that birth.

Scientology teaches that a natural quiet birth is much better for the baby, but I was in too much pain with Jessica and asked for some relief. I remember getting to the hospital and asking the nurse if I could walk around to help speed up Jeremy's birth because my first baby had taken so long. After she examined me, she said I was fully dilated and the baby was coming very soon so she called the doctor immediately. I thought, wow, that's the way to have a baby. There wasn't even any time for them to put an IV in me.

Jim and I were very happy that now we had a girl and a boy. They were almost three years apart. I loved being a mom and loved my two children very much. Jim loved our children too and enjoyed being a dad. I got a six-week leave from work after Jeremy's birth and then had to go back to work. We didn't want to put our children in daycare because it was too costly, so I worked nights and Jim worked days. Being a mom of two young children and working nights was really hard on me. My mom bought another house and we all moved in together.

Then my friend Rob and I decided to get an in-home family day care license. I could make more money and be home with my children. Rob was the son of my mom's good friend Rosie. He loved kids and had his daycare college units like I did. Mom and Rosie suggested that Rob and I partner up and get our own daycare. I loved the idea and so did he. I knew Rob was a really nice guy. He was about ten years younger than I and I could tell he'd be good with kids. Rob and I got our license and opened a family daycare licensed for twelve children. We ran it for about a year. It was better hours for me than working at night at the grocery store. I loved being able to be with my kids all day and not have some other person taking care of them.

Our daycare was not a Scientology daycare. I was not that involved with Scientology at that time. I was busy taking care of my children. Rob and I got along great and enjoyed our business. Jessica was now three-and-a-half and Jeremy was one. I loved having weekends off to be with my family. Jim and I took our kids to the lake on the weekends in the summer. Jeremy also went up to the lake when he was a baby and went to the Lakeport Labor Day Fair, too. Jeremy loved going in the boat just like Jessica had. Our kids loved the lake and I loved spending time at the lake house with my dad and stepmom and my half-sister and half-brother.

Family meant so much to me. The weekends that we didn't go to the lake we did family things with my mom. We would have Sunday dinners and invite my grandma over for dinner. We'd take the kids to the park or the zoo. My kids were raised in a loving atmosphere. Their grandparents spoiled them a lot and they loved it.

After working the daycare for about a year, I got a phone call from Jean. She was the owner of Los Gatos Academy, which was a Scientology school. She had heard I went to school to be a P.E. teacher and she was looking for one. I told her that I didn't have my credentials and she said in a private school it wasn't necessary. I told her no at first because of my daycare and partner Rob. Finally, I talked with him about it and said I was really interested in the job opportunity. I told him that I had always wanted to be a P.E. teacher. We worked it out and Rob went back to school and I took the job at Los Gatos Academy. I wouldn't run into any Sea Org recruiters there, but once again I had put myself back into a Scientology environment.

Chapter Five

Working at the Scientology School

In 1995, when my children were two and four-and-a-half years old, I became the P.E. teacher at Los Gatos Academy. I taught P.E. to all the grades from kindergarten through high school. That's how several Scientology schools worked at the time, offering their education from the beginning of school through pre-college. Jeremy was in the preschool, which was not specifically a Scientology preschool. The preschool was on the campus, but separated from the upper school. Jeremy started in the room for two-year-olds. Since Jessica was almost five, she started in kindergarten. I loved being able to work at the school my kids attended.

After I'd served a few months as the P.E. teacher, my boss Jean asked if I could help out in the afternoon in the preschool because they were short-staffed. So mornings I taught P.E. and afternoons I worked in the preschool. It was hard on me because I had to have different lesson plans for all the different ages of the upper-school kids. As it turned out, I preferred working with the preschool children. Jean recognized this. She found another person to teach P.E. and she offered me the Preschool Director job. Her previous director had given notice and Jean thought I would make a great director. I took the position. My husband wanted our kids to go to a Scientology school and since this school went from preschool up through high school, my taking the director job made Jim happy. He had told me that he never wanted our kids to attend a regular public school. I was simply happy I could work at the school where my children were.

I did well as the new preschool director. I started with two classrooms, a two-year-old room and a room for younger kids, a total of about twenty students. When I quit six years later, I had grown the preschool to about ninety students. By then it included a two-year-old room, a three-year-old room, and a classroom for three- and four-year-olds. I had four to five teachers and an assistant director.

I enjoyed the preschool. Most of the teachers were not Scientologists, but the owner of the school insisted that the preschool teachers had to take some basic Scientology courses. I remember they had to take the Ups and Downs in Life course and How to be a Successful Parent. Many of the non-Scientology teachers I interviewed did not want to take these classes. I told my boss the problem, so she decided to reward them with a pay increase when they completed the classes. After we put that into the hiring process, most of the potential teachers would agree to it. The majority of the teachers I hired just did the minimum Scientology classes and never went on to do more in Scientology. I never pressured my teachers to become Scientologists. In fact, I hated the pressure I would get from different Scientologists to try to get my teachers interested in doing more Scientology.

My teachers really liked me and we all became great friends. I was required to attend the staff meetings with the upper school and all the Scientology teachers. We had to keep graphs with statistics for each week. My three statistic graphs were how many enrolled preschool students there were, how many pieces of promo I handed out each week, and how many new students I got enrolled. It was a lot of pressure. We had to hold up our graphs in front of all the staff at weekly meetings. I was very good at my job and usually did quite well, but if one of our graphs was headed downward, we had to do a lower ethics condition and that wasn't fun.

During my first year working at the school, I had seen an alarming situation happening right before my eyes when I walked into the office to check my mail slot. I found a coworker crying. I approached her and asked her why she was upset. I'll never forget her response: "My daughter is joining the Sea Organization and there is nothing I can do to stop it!"

I thought to myself, *Wow, that is strange!* Why would she be unable to stop her fifteen-year-old daughter from signing a billion-year contract with the Sea Org? I tried to talk with her more in detail, but she clearly wanted to be alone. It bothered me all day. My attention would not get off what I had just seen.

I went home that day and shared the incident with Jim. I told him that I would never approve of or allow our children to join the Sea Org. I had a really bad feeling about it and had heard horror stories of parents never seeing their children again.

Our opinions on this matter differed. His stepson from his first marriage, Chris Leake, had joined the Sea Org at the age of twelve or thirteen and went to work "Over the Rainbow." I'm pretty sure that "Over the Rainbow" was what they then called the Scientology installation at Hemet, near Los Angeles, which became known in Scientology as Gold. This meant that Chris had gone to a place within Scientology with an extremely high level of security (a secret place) and his mother was not even aware of his location. I couldn't imagine how his mother felt. I couldn't do that. Incidentally, Chris ended up marrying L. Ron Hubbard's granddaughter, Roanne, in the early '90s. I'm not sure of the exact year, but when they visited us, both my kids had been born, and they were already married.

What Chris did was not uncommon. While working at the Los Gatos Academy Preschool, I noticed a lot of the high school kids in the upper part of Los Gatos Academy left and joined the Sea Org. I remember the names Jessica Feshbach, Harrison and Allie Luoma; and Harrison and Allie were younger than high-school age. Their parents joined, too. There were many others. It was so gross how the Sea Org recruiters preyed on the kids at the Scientology school. I hated it. Children should be left alone so they can get an education. I was very concerned about my own kids when they reached high school. I did not want them recruited for the Sea Org at all.

During the six years I worked at the school, Jim and I would take our kids to the lake in the summer for the weekend. Jessica, Jeremy and I would go on a special trip with my mom for a week over the 4th of July. Jim didn't go on this yearly trip with us. The 4th of July was also my mom's birthday and we couldn't wait to celebrate her big day. We would all stay at a fun place called Konocti Harbor Resort and Spa. It was located across the lake from my dad and stepmom's place. We always had a blast and wonderful quality family time. I had so much stress working at the school that I counted the days to our favorite vacation. My kids adored my mom, whom they called Nonie. Jim and I and the kids would also spend every Memorial Day weekend and Labor Day weekend with my dad and stepmom at their lake house, the same house I had known since I was a baby. This was truly the best of times.

During the winter when I was working at the school we would go snowboarding at Lake Tahoe. The kids and I loved to snowboard. Their dad didn't board with us. I don't remember what Jim did. My dad and stepmom treated us to Tahoe and we would stay at the Embassy Suites. My parents got us our own suite and that was special. My dad skied with us and we had a blast! I never had much extra money to do things like this, so we really appreciated what my dad and stepmom did.

Jim and I struggled financially throughout our entire marriage. In 2001, I decided to leave my husband. After thirteen years of being in an unhappy marriage, I just couldn't do it anymore. I was not in love with Jim and didn't think I could stay in the marriage just for the kids. I wanted my kids to have a happy mom. The final straw for me was when Jim called me at work from the bank. He wanted to get a loan against our house for thousands of dollars so he could get more Scientology counseling. He told me that this next Scientology action he was going to do would handle his finances. I told him we couldn't do that and anyway my dad and stepmom were signers on the house with us and he couldn't get a loan without their signatures. Thank God for that or we would have probably been on the streets after taking that loan. I was so sick of living the way we did and all Jim wanted was to do more Scientology, which cost a lot of money that we didn't have.

I remember when I asked Jim for a divorce he said to me, "You're not really a Scientologist!" Now I look back at his comment and think of it as a compliment. He also told me, "You will never find anyone that loves you!" When he said that, I thought to myself, *Oh yes I will, and he will be wonderful.*

Jim insisted that we do the 2-D co-audit counseling again. He even got John Allender, the Mission Holder of San Jose at that time, to call me in to see him. John ordered me to go to the Flag Land Base in Florida, the main Scientology installation, and do the 2-D co-audit with Jim. He said that Flag was ordering it and that I couldn't say no. I was required to fly to Florida and pay for accommodations. Allender was very upset with me because I told him I couldn't go and he said I *had* to go. I walked out of his office. I did not like him at all. John Allender was also my course supervisor back when I was taking Scientology classes when I was in my teens and I felt extremely intimidated by him.

I never did go to Flag to do the action, but Jim still pressured me to do it. I did agree to do it at the San Jose Mission where I was taking services, and I hated doing it again. I told myself this time I was going to be strong and not be manipulated to stay in my unhappy, miserable marriage.

After we completed the action, I still wanted a divorce. John Allender tried to convince me that it was really hard out there as a single parent. I was getting the feeling that John was trying to persuade me to stay with Jim. It's interesting how many times John Allender was trying to control me. Little did I know what was ahead with John and me. I told him that I would be just fine.

I quit working at the Scientology school and went to work for my mom at the end of year 2000. I gave my boss at the school a month's notice. She was very upset that I was quitting and said to me, "So you're just going to be into bodies," which was a reference to my mom's nutritionist business. I was going to help people get in shape, eat right, and lose weight, and feel better about themselves. The month I was at the school after I gave notice was awful. My boss was cold to me and so were a few of the other staff members who knew I was leaving.

Only a few people knew I was quitting because there is a Scientology policy on leaving a workplace. Part of the policy is you cannot tell other staff members you are leaving, and if you do you get thrown in a lower ethics condition. I had learned that lesson before, so I kept it quiet.

I was so happy to be back working for my mom at Dee's Diet Counseling. I had worked for her before I moved to Illinois and it was great to be back. It was also great to change my life so that it wasn't about Scientology every waking moment of every day.

Chapter Six

A New Life and a New Husband

After Jim and I separated, I removed my children from the Los Gatos Academy and placed them in public school. As a single mother, I could no longer afford the steep prices of the private Scientology school. Jim was not happy with my pulling our kids out of the Academy, but he couldn't afford the high prices to pay for the school either. The Los Gatos tuition was around $625 per child in 2001. I was trying to pay for my house mortgage, the school, food, and basic bills. I couldn't do it for long. I was also concerned that if I kept my kids in a Scientology school the Sea Org recruiters would go after them. I wanted my kids to be well-rounded and have friends outside of Scientology. I didn't want them to be esoteric in their beliefs like their dad.

Jim always wanted our kids to only hang out with Scientology kids. We had neighbors who had two sweet girls named Tiffani and Brittani. Jim didn't like our kids to hang out with them. We argued about this over and over. I also knew how good I had done when I went to college and got away from Scientology's study technology. I felt my kids would do better and get a better education like I had.

One day something interesting happened at my new job. Mom transferred a potential client over to me because she had a waiting list and I had a few openings. I took the call and it was C.R. Hodgson. He wanted to get some more information on our nutrition counseling. He had been referred by his boss at the company where he worked. Mom was diet counseling his boss and several other employees from the company. I told CR about our program and he scheduled an appointment to come in and start.

I met my future husband on February 1, 2001. I didn't know on that day that he was the man I had been searching for all my life. I was still married to Jim, and CR was married, too. Nevertheless, there was something there from the beginning. He wasn't an older man. When he came in he filled out his medical form, I looked it over and saw that he was born in 1963, the same year as me. In fact, we were only five days apart. I was the older one.

I asked him what exercise he liked to do and he said he used to love to water-ski. I asked where he had done that and he said Clear Lake. I couldn't believe it. CR had been raised up at the lake on the weekends when he was little just like me. In fact, his lake house was only a few miles from my lake house. Once we figured that out, he said that he used to water-ski in front of my house because the water was smoother over there.

I told him that I used to water-ski in front of his house because I thought the water was smoother by his house. We had probably crossed paths many times. CR even went to the Lakeport County Fair like I did and we both loved the ride The Flying Bobs. We had probably been in line together. We ended up chatting about all the fun times we both had at the lake, then we got him started on his healthy eating plan. CR was a great client and did very well on the program. He lost over forty pounds. We became friends and as time went on we saw each other go through our difficult divorces.

I was divorced in December 2002. During the time after my divorce, I started dating again and that was very strange for me. I dated non-Scientology guys as I didn't like any of the single Scientology men around where I lived. I dated two men before I actually dated CR and each relationship only lasted a short while. I was determined not to settle for just anyone again and knew that both of these men were not for me. I was determined to find my true love and have a wonderful relationship filled with fun, love, and romance. I was going to find my real soulmate. I wanted the happy ending of those love stories I had read years ago. I knew true love was out there somewhere.

After CR's divorce in 2003, I began playing matchmaker and set him up with my best friend. They had a date, but they only liked each other as friends. I told CR that I had many single friends and would try to find him a good match. He was my client for a couple of years and became a good friend, so I knew him well. I told my girlfriends that CR was a great guy. He was aware I was dating a guy that he knew through work and he told me that this guy was a womanizer who went to bars to pick up younger women. I was so happy that CR shared that with me.

After breaking up with my boyfriend right before Thanksgiving 2004, I was telling my mom I didn't know what to do because I was invited to a client's

Christmas party and I was originally going with my now ex-boyfriend. Mom suggested that I ask CR. She said he would be perfect to take to the party. So I took her advice and asked him if he would like to go to a Christmas party with me just as friends. I stressed the *friends* part since he was also my client.

CR said yes. The week before we went to the party, he asked me to go shopping with him to help him find a dressy shirt to wear. The week before we went shopping he came in for his nutrition visit and it was awkward for us. I thought to myself, *how come I am acting so nervous with CR? I have known him for a long time.* I gave him my address and he picked me up at my house on a Saturday afternoon, December 5, 2004. *This is not a date, just friends going shopping*, I told myself. We went to Santana Row, a small mall near my house, and then we got a bite to eat at Chili's restaurant nearby. Throughout our conversation at dinner the light bulb switched on for me.

At that moment, everything changed.

CR was telling me about how he loved going to Clear Lake when he was little and as he continued on with his fun memories I thought to myself, *OMG, I think I really like this guy. What was I doing setting him up with my girlfriends!*

Things changed for me from that moment on. I started thinking about CR and it was different now. He dropped me off after dinner and we shook hands, but I was feeling a lot more than that. The following Saturday, December 12, 2004, CR picked me up at my house. He arrived with a beautiful bouquet of flowers. I was surprised and thought it was so sweet. We had a nice visit on our way to the party and found out more things that we had in common. I couldn't believe how I was now feeling toward this man. I was starting to get butterflies in my stomach.

We had a great time at the party and were the last couple to leave. He hugged me goodnight, then called me the following day and asked if I wanted to go to his office Christmas party. I didn't hesitate one bit. I couldn't stop thinking about CR and how much I really liked him. It was so different for me, because we had been friends for several years. I had never dated a guy before this that I was good friends with first.

We had a wonderful time at his Christmas party.

A few days later, he invited me to his brother's birthday party. I remember this night very well. It was our third date and before we walked into the party he kissed me. That kiss blew me away! I couldn't believe this was happening. I felt like I was reading one of my love stories all over again, but this was reality.

CR and I were inseparable from that day on. We spent Christmas together and then my mom and stepdad, Val, invited us to Santa Cruz for New Year's weekend. After New Year's Eve, my children met CR and they really liked him. He and I took Jessica and Jeremy and CR's son Peter snowboarding at Lake Tahoe. We all had a great time. Jessica, Jeremy, and I snowboarded and Peter and CR skied.

A few months after CR and I started dating, I got pressure from some folks where I was taking Scientology classes to ask CR if he wanted to do a personality test and come down and check out the place. I asked him and he agreed. I took him down to the San Jose mission and he took the test. After he got his results, they got him to take the Communication Course and said that he could take it with me. CR said he would like to do that, because then we could be together in the same class and learn more about communication. We started the course that week and had a lot of fun doing it.

After we finished the course, the Scientology registrar closed him for his next step, which was the "How to be a Successful Parent" course. CR quickly learned that when you start Scientology they don't want you to stop after the first class. A person called the registrar is in charge of making sure both new Scientologists and old Scientologists continue on up the Bridge to Freedom, and if you take one course you're considered a Scientologist within the organization.

The "Bridge" is a gradient scale of levels a Scientologist progresses upward to the top to reach spiritual freedom. The registrar said the next course would help CR with parenting skills. He was a great dad to Peter and I don't think he needed much help in that area, but since he was previously divorced CR probably thought, *why not*. After he finished that course, we did the Purification Rundown together, a regimen designed to supposedly remove all the toxins from your system that were impeding your spiritual progress.

CR and I loved being together every day but not so much the sauna regimen. We had to schedule three to five hours to be in the sauna, including exercise and extensive vitamins daily. This rundown was supposed to allow us to think more clearly and not have the effect of residual drugs stored in the body. Truth was, we just enjoyed all the time we got to spend together. I'd already done this Purification sauna regimen three prior times and I hated sweating in the sauna, but I did it to hang out with CR.

We never missed a day. We finished the Purification Rundown and then the registrar got CR to do the first auditing step in Scientology, which was called Life Repair. This was an action done one-on-one with a Scientology counselor and the end result was to repair one's life from the troubles the person had suffered. I noticed CR didn't seem that excited about doing it. As the weeks went on, he seemed less and less enthused about this action. He told me he finished but shared with me that he really didn't like it and he thought that Scientology could use the auditing against a person since they find out all this private information about the individual. I told him I understood and never told the folks where I took my classes what CR had told me, because I knew they would pressure me to get him to come down and talk to them about it. I told CR that it was okay with me that he didn't want to do any more auditing and that I would never pressure him.

CR finally decided to do the Dianetics course just so they would stop bothering him. He didn't like that course at all. He said he wanted to do courses with me, but they insisted that he do this course which we could not do together. He felt like they wanted to keep us apart and didn't like that. I was in the Dianetics course as well, but we had to do it separately and I hated that. CR hated it so much he just got too busy with work and I told them he was too tired at night to go to class. Pat, the Ethics Officer, would talk to me all the time to try to get CR back on course. Every time, I told Pat he was too busy at work and exhausted at night.

The following Memorial Day weekend in 2005, CR and I took all the kids to the lake. He hadn't been up to Clear Lake since he was twenty years old. He was so happy to be back. He took me by his family's old lake house on a jet ski. It was only a five-minute ride. Later, CR water-skied and kicked my butt. I learned he was a fantastic slalom water-skier. I also thought I was pretty good at ping pong until I played against CR. He won every game.

On July 11, 2005, CR proposed to me at the top of Hopland, the mountain we drove over to get to the lake. He pulled off the road and said he wanted to show me the beautiful sunset. I had no idea he was going to propose. We were simply taking in the gorgeous sunset and he said he was going to go back to the car and get some water. He came back and asked me to marry him. I was so happy and said yes right away. I knew that we were soul mates and I had found my true love that I'd been looking for all my life. We got in the car and I called my mom and Grandma. They were both really excited for us. We then got to the lake and shared the news with my dad and stepmom and they too were really happy for us. After the weekend, we got back home to San Jose and shared our news with our children and all of them were happy. We spent the rest of the summer going up to the lake on the weekends. At the end of the summer, we came up with the wedding date—March 4, 2006. Making wedding plans kept me quite busy. We decided to have a Black and White wedding and had two hundred and twenty-five people on the guest list.

Fall came around and all the kids were back in school. CR's son Peter was in the middle of Jessica and Jeremy age-wise. CR had moved in with me over the summer. Our kids were with us on the same weeks. My custody with Jessica and Jeremy was sixty percent and their dad had them forty percent of the time. CR had Peter fifty percent of the time. All three kids played sports in public school and were doing well in their classes.

After growing up in a Scientology school, Jessica and Jeremy had to transition to the different setting, but adjusted rather well after a few months. I was happy to see that my kids were meeting other kids besides just Scientologists. Jessica stayed busy studying hard, getting A's and B's and playing on a soccer team. Jeremy was doing well in school and excelling in his karate class.

When Jeremy started in public school in fourth grade, he was behind on his reading level. This kind of surprised me because the Scientology school would brag how advanced they were compared to public school students. The public school fourth-grade teacher and I worked hard to catch Jeremy up to his proper grade level. He also played ice hockey and baseball. Jeremy and Jessica were both very active and enjoyed many sports, including water-skiing and snowboarding.

Our wedding day was everything I could have dreamed of. All our kids were in the wedding. It was a beautiful event and I was a very happy bride. Now I knew I had married the love of my life. We went to Carmel for our honeymoon and I felt the joy and the passion I had never known before. I was head-over-heels about my new husband.

The summer after our wedding was fun, too. We spent lots of family time together at the lake. Being in public school gave my children the summers off to spend more time with their family. In contrast, the Scientology school was year-round. My kids loved the summers off like I had when I was younger. We would go to the lake house most weekends in the summer and take a couple of weeks of vacation, too. Their grandma, my mom, whom they called Nonie, still took us to the lake for 4th of July week. We always stayed at Konocti Resort. The kids and I looked forward to this one-week vacation with their Nonie every year. We started counting the days several months beforehand.

On the way there, we would sing songs and talk about how much fun the previous summers had been. When we got to the lake, we always had the same motel room. It was on the end upstairs and had a lake view. The air conditioner was noisy, but we loved it. We were on a budget so we brought our cooler full of food and ate at the restaurant for lunch and dinner. We would bribe the kids with Beanie Babies if they didn't argue. Oh boy, did that work. We played ping pong all day, swam in the pool, played pee wee golf, and went to the arcade. This was the best family vacation ever with our Nonie. We always had a blast!

Nonie would treat us to concerts. We saw Vince Gill, Willie Nelson, and many others. Jessica and Jeremy loved going to kids camp, too. These were truly great bonding times and we would be so sad when it was time to go home.

I remember the last Konocti trip we all took. Jessica was fifteen and Jeremy was twelve. We were sitting in the hot tub and Jessica was sharing with us that she wanted to be a veterinarian. My mom and I were so proud of her for getting such good grades in school. She had her dreams laid out right in front of her. We had even visited Chico State together to see if she would like to go there. She was a very determined girl who had a bright future in front of her!

Life can change overnight, though. The week after we got back from our last Konocti trip, an unexpected nightmare with my kids began!

Chapter Seven

Jessica Gets Recruited

In 2006, just a few months after my wedding to CR, my parental rights began to be violated. Jessica was fifteen and preparing for her first semester of her sophomore year of high school. She was receiving all A's and B's, had many friends, and was looking forward to college. When my kids left the Scientology school for public school, they were not at the Scientology mission much in the evening. Their dad paid for them to take a few small Scientology classes and both kids complained how they didn't want to go and I totally understood. I would tell Jim that they had a lot of homework to do in the evenings and being on Scientology course at night was too hard on them.

I gave Jessica some of the tips I had learned about how to study in college. I think it helped her not get into those long chains of looking up every definition in a word. I was careful not to talk critically about Scientology study tech to my kids, in case they might tell their dad. I didn't need him or Scientology hounding me. I loved seeing how well both my kids were doing away from Scientology. They always had their friends come over, mostly friends from public school, but they did stay in touch with their Scientology friends, too.

One week after we got back from our Konocti vacation, before Jessica's sixteenth birthday, Scientology recruiters manipulated my daughter to join staff working for Scientology. Her father took her down to the Los Gatos Organization on a Sunday afternoon where he was taking Scientology classes. I had no idea he was taking her down there. She told me she was just going to go visit her dad for a bit. Jim lived only a few blocks from us so she could walk over to see him. After reviewing a staff recruiting film and speaking with recruiters, without my knowledge or permission, she came home and did not tell me where she had been. I had no idea she had been recruited. That next day, a Monday, her father brought her over to my workplace and he waited in the parking lot in his truck. Jessica asked if she could talk to me. She told me she wanted to go on staff at Los Gatos Org and that she wanted to do so real soon. I was shocked and I got really upset.

"What do you mean, and what about school?" I said.

"I will get my GED and then join staff."

"There is no way I'm agreeing to this," I replied. "Absolutely not!" I started sobbing.

Her response was to start repeating the alarming propaganda that the film she saw the day before had suggested. Essentially, it was a film demonizing psychiatry and implied that public schools had a large influence on psychiatric and street drugs. The film said that public school and the environment it provided were unsafe. After reviewing this film, Jessica wanted to drop out of school and obtain her GED, in addition to joining staff at the Church of Scientology. My fifteen-year-old daughter, a minor, was being recruited to put her education aside and work for the "church."

I was shocked by her sudden change of behavior. I told her again absolutely not! I said that once she turned eighteen she could make that decision, but I preferred she go to college first. My mom saw that I was crying; her office was across from mine and she was on the phone when this conversation was taking place. She ended her call and came in my office to see what was wrong. I was hysterical about what Jessica had just told me and tried to tell my mom. Mom asked Jessica to come into her office and talk. I just stayed at my desk crying. I thought, *this cannot be happening*! My biggest nightmare that I had tried to keep my kids away from was happening. How was I going to stop this? I wanted my daughter to finish high school and college so she would never have to endure what I went through.

Jessica left without saying goodbye to me. I asked my mom where she was going and was told she was just going to the bathroom. After a few minutes, I got up to see if she was coming back in and noticed the bathroom key was not missing. Jessica never went to the bathroom; she just said that so she could leave. I'm sure she was coached by Scientology and her dad to just leave if it didn't go well, which I'm sure they knew it wouldn't. I talked with my mom about what had just happened and we both were utterly shocked. Just a week before, we had all been on vacation and Jessica said she loved school and really wanted to go to college and maybe become a vet. How could Scientology and her father manipulate her this fast to give up on her dreams? It was mind-boggling, to say the least.

The next nine months were a living hell. I was adamantly against Jessica's joining staff, a feeling that was relayed to the church. I would not budge and I had Jessica continue on in her public school. She was very upset with me for not going along with Scientology's plan for her. This whole situation put a ton of stress on our mom-and-daughter relationship. She started getting poor grades in her public school and when she would see me she would look at me with hate in her eyes. I was so upset that Scientology was turning my daughter against me. Before this happened, Jessica and I were very close and had many wonderful times together. We loved watching "Gilmore Girls" on TV, going shopping, and just hanging out.

CR thought the whole thing was crazy. He believed strongly in education just like I did and supported my decision to want to keep my daughter in public school so she could get a proper education and go to college. While attending counseling within the church myself, I had been pulled from what I was working on and put into "interrogation" counseling. The Church demanded to know "who" did not agree with Jessica joining staff, even after I told them repeatedly that I was the only one who did not want her to join staff.

In Scientology, they believe strongly that there is a Suppressive Person behind every trouble. At the San Jose Mission where I was getting the counseling, they couldn't get me to give in so they got another counselor to see if that could crack me, but that didn't work either. I also had to pay for this extensive "security"-type counseling, all because I wouldn't agree with them about taking my daughter out of her school that she was winning in to work for Scientology. This cost me thousands of dollars. I think I paid around $2,600 an intensive, which was twelve-and-a-half hours of counseling. That meant I was paying two hundred and eight dollars an hour for counseling I didn't even want to do. This went on for months. I think I spent around $10,000 on this interrogative counseling. It was totally insane, but since I was a Scientologist, I had to do it.

When the "church" couldn't find their "who"—the person putting the anti-Scientology ideas in my head that they were certain had to be there—they put me in extensive Chaplain meetings with my daughter and her father. The Scientology Chaplain is the person you see if there are familial troubles. This went on for a couple more months. After all the pressure I had from Scientology and her father, I finally gave in. We agreed that Jessica would go to a Scientology school and get her high school diploma before joining staff. I thought this would buy us some time—like a few years—and hopefully Jessica would change her mind about joining staff.

Surprisingly, Jessica got her non-accredited diploma when she was sixteen. I was livid with how they had planned this whole thing behind my back. I felt totally betrayed by Scientology and my daughter's dad. She graduated only a few months after she attended the Scientology school. I was still trying to persuade her not to join staff, but she did so against my wishes. She signed a five-year contract and was told that if she broke the contract she would owe a "freeloader debt" for staff training and other "services" she received while on staff. She would have to pay off her debt before she was allowed to do any more Scientology services.

I reminded Jessica of this and she said, "I'm not going to leave, Mom."

I wanted to tell her that she was making the biggest mistake of her life, just like I had when I was her age. I took her to Chevy's for dinner to discuss this before I agreed to sign her staff contract. I shared what had happened with me and how I regretted it and wished I would have stayed in school. My words didn't matter. Jessica was so convinced by the staff recruiters that whatever I said was moot. She was headstrong on joining staff. I started crying in the restaurant. Jessica got mad at me and said I was embarrassing her. I was beside myself and didn't know what else I could do. I felt like I couldn't win; she was too far gone and committed.

After Jessica was on staff for several weeks, she was sent to Florida for training. She was there for three months, battling homesickness, before deciding it was not for her and she came home. She then worked at the Los Gatos organization for a couple more months but again came to the determination that she didn't want to be on staff any longer. She had to have special "interrogating counseling" and do specific "conditions" before she left. When she left staff she had accumulated a $13,000 debt, most likely from the counseling she was ordered to get because she wanted to leave!

I think this debt was accumulated at Flag when she was there doing her training. Since she didn't want to be on staff, they made her do security check counseling and that is where that huge debt came from. She was in Florida less than three months.

Flag auditing was much more expensive than auditing elsewhere. I never got the details on costs because it was all very secretive and Jessica was pretty closed-mouth with me. Even though she was my minor child, I could get barely any information from anyone in Scientology about what had happened with her. It was completely asinine.

On top of her $13,000 debt at sixteen years old, she had to do "amends" to the organization! She had to do ethics condition formulas from Treason on up to Normal and one hundred hours of amends. Jessica was still very secretive about all this, I think because they told her not to "put it on anyone's lines," which meant not to tell anyone. She needed to only talk to her "ethics terminal" over this matter while she was doing conditions and amends—that being the person who approved or disapproved of her progress through the amends. She did share with me that she had to clean the bathrooms with a toothbrush and I got really upset, which caused her to worry over sharing that with me. The whole thing was totally weird and secretive just like when she had been recruited for staff. I hated it!

So Jessica had to work over one hundred hours to get back in "good standing" with the so-called "church" just because she wanted to go back to school. A couple of weeks went by of this crap then the Los Gatos Org told Jessica that they had a "Minor Rates Special." This meant they needed money, as usual. If Jessica could pay off her debt in full in three days, they would knock her debt down to six thousand dollars.

I think someone knew that if they told her they would cut the debt down it would make it more of a motivation for Jessica to find someone to lend her the money. I heard that my Scientology Case Supervisor (supervisor of my auditing), Lynda Allender, was involved in helping Jessica get the cycle done. The registrars would stop at nothing until they got their money for the org. All they cared about was how much money they could bring in and they would do that in any way possible, ethical or not. How sick is that!

My mom ended up giving Jessica the money. Meanwhile, the Scientologists who assisted her most likely received a commission on Jessica's debt. Her father and Lynda Allender worked together on getting this done.

After Jessica left staff, I helped her get a job at a preschool and get her started on her Preschool classes at West Valley Junior College where I had gone. I was so happy to see her going to junior college and liking school again. Jessica was doing much better at this point.

It appeared that Jessica might have learned a lesson, and after the awful staff and debt experience, she would have a chance at a normal life, but Scientology never gives up on their continual recruiting. Next up for abuse was my son Jeremy, and it would be an even more traumatic experience.

Chapter Eight

Jeremy Gets Recruited for the Sea Org

In 2007, Jessica was seventeen, working at a preschool and taking junior college classes in the evening. Jeremy was fourteen and beginning his freshman year in public high school and actively trying out for the football team. After school, Jeremy was involved in karate. He loved it and was doing quite well. He was getting his Blue Belt at this time. I would take him to karate and stay to watch him. He mentioned that he would like to work there when he was a little older. We went to karate three to four times a week. His father would bash his karate place and tell Jeremy that it wasn't a very good studio. Jim tended to denigrate everything I tried to do with my kids. I think he would only have been happy if I had them doing only Scientology actions.

On the weekends during this time, Jeremy, CR, and I would go dirt biking to Hollister Hills about an hour away from our house and at Carnegie State Vehicular Recreation Area near Livermore. We went riding on most weekends that I had my kids. Jessica occasionally joined us. Riding was a great family sport and we all loved it. We got Jeremy his own bike and later got him a bigger one.

Jeremy got on the football team and I was so excited. I encouraged him to be in school sports. Unfortunately, during one of his practices he injured his foot and couldn't play for a while. Then, after a month in school, he told me that he didn't like public school anymore and wanted to attend the Scientology school his sister had attended. This conversation was eerily similar to the one I had had with Jessica not long before. I was beginning to suspect an entirely new nightmare was about to begin.

I recalled my conversation with my son when he saw what Jessica had gone through dropping out of school, joining staff, and leaving with a huge debt. Jeremy told me, "I will never do that, Mom!" I thought maybe my fears were unfounded. After all, he wasn't even taking any Scientology courses or had any real interest in going down to Scientology.

Still, I felt his dad was a huge influence on Jeremy wanting to drop out of public school, because Jim always told me when we were married that he hated public school and that his kids would never go there. I told Jim I would not pay for the Scientology school and that Jeremy was doing fine in public school and did like it and that I couldn't understand how this all changed so quickly. Jim said he would pay for it so his son could go to Scientology school. I thought there was no way Jim could pay for that—he had a hard enough time staying current with the child support he owed me.

I fought the whole thing again now with my second child and didn't win. I had to go to the Ethics Officer and I couldn't stand the pressure the Scientologist put me through. After Jeremy attended the Scientology school, his interest in sports declined and he began taking Scientology classes. Jeremy didn't even want to dirt bike with us like he used to. His interest in karate was diminishing as well. I noticed Jeremy seemed more private and didn't want to hang out with me and CR that much. I was worried that I was losing my son like I had lost my daughter.

Jim was having financial troubles as usual, and after Jeremy was at the Scientology school for a couple of months Jeremy said that his dad couldn't afford to pay the whole tuition and that he was going to switch to a half-day schedule and then go to Scientology the other half of the day and take classes. I think this whole thing was planned out ahead of time behind my back. I fought back and lost another battle. Again, I had to go see the Ethics Officer and got pulled off my auditing because I would not agree. The pressure was just too much, so I felt I had no choice but to let Jeremy do what he wanted. Jeremy had a couple of friends at the new Scientology school that he knew from his old Scientology school. Jeremy's friend, Max, went to the Scientology school and his mom was the Mission Holder of a different San Jose mission than the one I went to. The kids who went to Jeremy's new Scientology school were mostly Scientologists.

So when Jeremy turned fifteen, he was still part-time at the school and the rest of the time at the Scientology center taking classes. He barely talked to CR and me about his Scientology classes. My son didn't seem to me to be very happy. I could tell a big difference from before when he went to public school, played with his friends, and participated in all his sports. We tried to get Jeremy to go dirt biking with us and he would, but only once in a while. I think those times that we could dirt bike together brought us closer.

Jeremy and I would also go to Chili's, his favorite place to eat, once a week and we would have mom-and-son time. Jessica and I would have our once-a-week dinner together, too. I tried hard to keep that going with my kids. Jeremy talked about the Sharks hockey team and dirt bikes most of the time we were together. Jessica talked about her college preschool classes and her job at the preschool. Jessica and I loved to snowboard so we talked about that, too.

In November 2008, I went to the hospital for knee replacement surgery. It was an extremely complicated procedure entailing four long days in the hospital. One week later, on a Friday night, while I was at home recovering from my surgery, my fifteen-year-old son attended a Sea Org recruiting event that his father took him to. It was Jim's weekend to have Jeremy and I did not know Jim had taken him there. Strangely, that evening, I had a worried feeling about my son, and I soon learned why! The following Sunday morning, Jeremy came over from his dad's to visit me and told me he wanted to join the Sea Org. That didn't go over very well.

At this time, I was in excruciating pain from my surgery and on high levels of pain medication and I was not functioning properly. Jeremy told me that joining the Sea Org was his sole purpose in his life and he was aware that it was a billion-year contract. He'd bought into the belief that one lives many lifetimes, comes back to a new body, and as such could continue his contract to the organization and the Church in the Sea Org.

I always thought that was totally crazy and said so! Jeremy said that he needed to leave in a couple of days. I was hysterical, distraught, and felt that I was truly on the verge of losing my mind. The pain and high dosages of Percocet (a strong narcotic pain pill) didn't help my state. I told him absolutely NOT! Jessica heard this and came to see what was wrong. She saw how upset I was and told me there was nothing she could do; that she was already in an upsetting situation with Scientology and she couldn't get in the middle of it.

I told Jeremy that he was not to join the Sea Org. He was a minor, a fifteen-year-old boy without the life experience to make such a profound decision. He left to go back to his dad's house. I frantically called my mom and explained to her what had just happened. She was extremely upset about the situation and after we hung up she drove over to Jim's house to talk with Jeremy. Jim wouldn't let Jeremy open the door, but my mom wouldn't leave so Jeremy finally let her in. She told her grandson that this was not okay to do especially because "your mom is not doing well right now and she is in a lot of pain."

She then told Jeremy that I said he could not join the Sea Org until he turned eighteen. Jeremy listened to my mom and she said he looked like he felt really bad for his actions. Jeremy agreed to not do this and Jim said to him, "Are you sure about that, son?"

Jeremy didn't answer and my mom left because the whole thing made her sick. She came over to see me and to help calm me down. I was relieved that she got Jeremy to see that what he was doing was not okay and that he could not join the Sea Org. I felt better and thanked my mom. She is always there for me no matter what. I love my mom more than anything.

Later that evening, Jeremy came back and continued to ask permission to join. Every part of me ached, reeled, and screamed from the mental and physical pain. The thought of me losing my son was unbearable! Seeing me in such distress, my husband tried to diffuse the situation by asking Jeremy to leave and to respect the decision of his mother.

Upon Jeremy's refusal to listen, my husband contacted Pat Wehner, who was the Ethics Officer and Scientology Mission Holder where I took services. Pat Wehner had taken over John Allender's Mission Holder position a few years before. Pat told CR there was nothing he could do about stopping Jeremy's recruitment and my husband told me what Pat had said. I had heard that before, from my daughter. My husband was really upset and he told Pat how he felt. He couldn't believe that Pat would not stop this and thought the whole thing was cruel and downright awful. I feel that this situation is what made my husband never want anything more to do with Scientology. He couldn't believe what was going on. My son was very persistent and acting like he rehearsed what he continually repeated to me. He wasn't even being himself. Jeremy finally went back to his dad's house because he could see I was emphatic about saying no and I think deep down he couldn't stand the pain and anguish he was causing me. In the following days, I was harassed by recruiters trying to persuade me to allow my son to join the Sea Org.

All of this wasn't helping my progress in Scientology and, most important, allowing me to recover from a traumatic surgery. Before my knee replacement, I had done some more Scientology counseling, which CR helped me finance. We got a loan for around $28,000 and I could never have done this without CR. My husband could see that I really wanted to do this and he was fine with helping me get the loan. CR was cool with me still doing Scientology, but I never told at the mission that my husband was not that excited about doing Scientology anymore because I knew they would pressure me to get him down there.

It was never a big deal to me that CR didn't want to be a Scientologist. I continued to make excuses for him that he was too busy, but they bugged me all the time to get him to come down. I hated the pressure. I made sure that I did my counseling in the afternoon and was only on course at night two times a week. I told the Scientology center that I needed to be home on some evenings to be with my children and my husband. I was always home on the weekends. They wanted me to commit to more, but I wouldn't. I loved spending time with my husband and my kids and they were my priority. Because I put my husband and kids first, my husband did not mind if I did my Scientology counseling and classes because it didn't interfere with our time. CR spent time with his son on the two nights I was at class and the nights I was with my kids.

As the Jeremy situation escalated, I contacted Pat Wehner to help me write up reports to Mark Warlick, the man in charge of Internal Scientology Legal Affairs at the Los Gatos Scientology Organization, where my kids had been recruited. Warlick's official title is DSA (Director of Special Affairs). My reports stated that as Jeremy Leake's mother, I was not allowing him to join the Sea Org and I wanted all recruiting to stop until he was eighteen. The church had their agenda, though; they wanted my son.

Because of all the stress, I was not physically healing properly. While at home, recruiters arrived and stood outside my living room window insisting that they talk to me. I told them to leave; that I couldn't talk and had to leave for physical therapy. The interaction really startled me. I couldn't stop shaking. My father arrived to take me to physical therapy just as the recruiters left, barely missing each other. I wanted to tell my father so badly about the situation of Scientology trying to take my son from me. But I knew if I didn't handle this internally with those people, I would get in big trouble with Scientology. If my father was aware of this he would have called the police on those recruiters.

Scientology insists that if there are problems, such as family problems, the individual only handles the problem within the Organization. Going outside the church to law enforcement, attorneys, and child services is forbidden. If a Scientologist does not handle the situation internally and goes outside for help, the Scientologist will get severe ethics actions to deal with.

After physical therapy, my dad brought me home and put me to bed and left. Within minutes, the recruiters were back, pounding on my door for at least fifteen minutes. I was frantic and frightened. I tried to call my mom but she was unavailable so I left a message and the recruiters pounding on my door was recorded on her work voicemail. I then called Pat Wehner and he verbally tried to calm me down. He did not want me to create a scene and cause bad PR for Scientology.

Although he lived right down the street, Pat did not come over to assist me. Seeing that the harassment and constant recruiting was harming my recovery, my lifelong friend Mari met with the two main recruiters, Gerald and Alexis, at a Starbucks. Mari tried to get them to understand my physical condition and state of mind. She got my drug list and details of my surgery, which included the information about my leg, basically the equivalent of being amputated and put back together.

The recruiters told her that they heard I was watching TV and that if I was able to watch TV then I was able to handle a Sea Org recruiting cycle of my son. The recruiters were cold and calculating; they were not stopping until they had my son, no matter what.

I shared this situation with my auditor, Julie, who would come over to my house and give me Scientology healing techniques called touch assists and other assists to try to help me with the pain. Scientology assists supposedly help one in pain without drugs. Julie would listen to my complaints and then change the subject back to my assist. I would tell her that I couldn't handle the stress of them recruiting my son and I would cry. She would continue to put my mind back on the assists.

I also called my Case Supervisor, Lynda Allender, and told her and she did the same thing, to refocus me on my assists. Neither one of them seemed to hear or care about what I was trying to tell them. It made me feel like it was my problem that I was against this recruitment and I needed to be focusing on healing. I thought, *how the heck can I heal with this going on*? I thought it was beyond awful what was happening in all areas. I would share this with my husband and he would get really upset and want to do something. I would tell him to please stay out of it because I didn't want him "wrong targeted" by Scientologists. I was the one against the recruiting but Scientology believes there is always another person influencing you.

Even with all best efforts, the recruiting did not cease or even slow down. In fact, they went to my parents' home twice late at night with Jeremy to get my mom to "handle" me and get me to allow Jeremy to join the Sea Org. They also showed up with my son at my mother's place of employment to talk to her again during a school day when my son was supposed to be in school.

After the Mission Holder, Pat Wehner, failed to assist my mother and me in our pleas to stop this insanity, my mother called our good friend Mari and met up with her to seek guidance in the situation. Mari, a smart person, figured out how to best protect me in my condition and helped me secure a doctor's note, which she then promptly delivered to Mark Warlick, the legal officer for the Los Gatos org. Before Mari picked up my letter, I called my doctor, being careful not to mention that it was Scientology causing me the stress. I knew if I was honest and told my doctor what was really going on, I would get in big trouble.

As Scientologists, we were forbidden to talk critically in any way about Scientology. I told my doctor that I was having a very difficult family situation and was under a lot of stress that was keeping me from healing. I said it had to do with my ex–husband and my kids, which was true. I just left out the Scientology recruiters and the manipulation Scientology staff was doing to try to take my son from me. I so much wanted to tell my doctor everything but I was scared.

He did write a letter that I was his patient and needed no stress for three months so that I could recover and heal from my knee surgery. Later, after the note had been delivered, Mari went to meet with the recruiters who had been pounding on my door. She wanted to tell them that she orchestrated the contact with my doctor and obtained the note to have this situation corrected once and for all. Before she was able to tell them what had occurred, however, she was told that whoever got the physician's note was a Suppressive Person! So she kept it quiet. If Mari had told the recruiters it was she who had gotten the doctor's letter, she would have probably been declared a Suppressive Person and the consequences would be getting kicked out of Scientology and losing all her family and friends that remained in Scientology.

With all the continual Scientology recruitment trying to take my son from me, my health was not improving. In fact, it was deteriorating and I was rushed back to the emergency room where I remained for ten hours. I had an ovarian cyst rupture and was diagnosed with pneumonia in addition to my knee, which was not healing from replacement surgery. A rupture of an ovarian cyst if not treated immediately can lead to death and I was admitted for three days. I think the doctor's letter finally had an effect for a short time after the recruiters heard I was hospitalized. In the following weeks, the recruiting did ease slightly and Jeremy and I began growing closer. Finally he told me he had changed his mind and no longer wanted to join the Sea Org.

Hearing those words filled me with such an immense amount of hope and joy! That joy was short-lived, however. Unbeknownst to me, the recruiting was continuing behind my back despite the many reports I had written to Mark Warlick insisting that the recruiting stop.

One evening I was with my son and I saw this worried expression on his face while he was looking down at a text on his phone. I asked him what was wrong. He said the recruiter Gerald was bugging him again. I was livid and called up Mark Warlick telling him to have it stop now.

Shortly thereafter, Jeremy came back to tell me that he did want to join the Sea Org and they promised him that he would continue his schooling, obtain his driver's license, and his orthodontic treatment would progress as scheduled. They promised him he could have his own computer and take trips to play golf, as well as enticed him with the attractive girls there, knowing how badly Jeremy wanted a nice girlfriend. They also promised me that I could talk to him anytime I wanted and he would be able to come home for his birthday and most major holidays.

I fought and fought against this and the constant begging and the coercion by the Church of Scientology. I felt hopeless and trapped. Jeremy continually would try to get me to let him go in the Sea Org and after I said no, he would go in the backyard and get right on the phone. He probably had to check in with Gerald the recruiter or his father, and they most likely further coached Jeremy on how to handle me. This went on for several days.

Ultimately, I felt the only way to keep my son and be able to maintain contact with him was to allow him to join the Sea Org. I felt I had no other choice; it was awful! I was bullied into doing this by the threat of disconnection. I was also still in a lot of pain with my botched knee replacement and looking at another surgery soon to fix it. I was very worried that if I refused, Scientology would manipulate my son to disconnect from me.

The recruiting within the organization is crude and filled with false promises and lies. These kids do not know what they are getting into. They are signing billion-year contracts without having even lived to adulthood! Children get robbed of their schooling, which prepares them for adult life choices. I just wanted both of my kids to have their proper schooling and go to college before they were forced into making choices that I knew would be devastating, but I lost those battles.

On May 4, 2009, Jeremy left for the Sea Org. I signed under mental duress a power of attorney and guardianship to Bob Wright and his wife Elyssa. Bob was Jeremy's uncle and worked very closely under David Miscavige, the leader of Scientology. Because Bob was Jeremy's uncle, I believed he would look after Jeremy's best interest and well-being while in the Sea Org. What I didn't understand fully at the time was that legally Bob was Jeremy's guardian but many of the decisions in Jeremy's life would be made by the "church," not Bob. I found out later that Bob was the international building construction manager for Scientology and spent most of his time away from Jeremy. I'm not sure if Bob's wife was around much either.

When a minor joins the S.O., the Sea Org makes the parent sign over guardianship. Since neither Jim, CR, nor I was going to be there with Jeremy, as a minor he had to have a guardian. Most S.O. kids do not have a family member there with them, so anyone is assigned as their guardian and it's a joke. The guardian does nothing. It's just a legality. Anyway, that's why I signed off for his uncle to be his guardian. Jim and Jeremy insisted on that.

I remember this day clearly. I had to drive down there to sign the contract in front of a notary. I felt totally manipulated and in a way forced to do this because I knew if I didn't I would probably lose my son at that moment to disconnection and I couldn't take that chance. I hated it! I felt like I was being made to give up my child and there was no other choice. Jim was there. He met me there and was more than willing to sign that damn contract. This whole thing made me feel like I was in a prison camp of some kind that took your kids away.

And it was about to get worse.

Chapter Nine

Jessica Takes the Sea Org Route

In the two weeks following Jeremy's recruitment, I was preparing for my second knee surgery to replace my initial knee replacement that had complications. I was missing my son terribly. During this time, Jessica went down to Los Angeles with her fiancé, Justin, and they were both heavily recruited to join the Sea Org while she was there. Jessica told me that she was going to Los Angeles with Justin to have fun and visit friends. I'm sure that's what Justin told her as well. Her fiancé wanted to join, but she didn't. The recruiters coerced her by screaming at her to join. They eventually wore her down and she did join under extreme pressure, but I did not know she had signed the billion-year contract for the Sea Org until she came back from her trip. They told her it was her only choice. I think my daughter felt pressured and trapped, especially knowing if she didn't join she would most likely lose her fiancé. Jessica shared how they recruited her after she had left the Sea Org.

While I was in the hospital, on my second day after surgery, Jessica visited and said goodbye to me and joined the Sea Org. She mentioned that she and Justin were going to get married in a couple of days so they could be together in the S.O. I was extremely distraught about not being there for my only daughter's wedding and losing her to the S.O. close to the same time my son had left, but she was eighteen and as an adult had the power to make that decision herself, no matter how against it I was.

Now I had lost both of my kids to this corrupt and cruel organization and Jessica's wedding was being planned while I was still in the hospital! I couldn't wrap my mind around a "religion" being so heartless.

I was so upset that the next day I went into shock. Luckily, my dad was there and he went to get help as he knew I was in trouble. He ran down the hallway yelling for help and the medical response team came and pulled me out of the shock. I felt like I almost died but I got a second chance. I ended up having to get a full blood transfusion. I decided that, since I made it, I was going to make some changes in my life.

Little did I know what was on the horizon for me.

On my fifth day post-op, I was released to my house that used to be blessed with the presence of my two children. I was incredibly grateful that at least I had my wonderful husband, my loyal dog to greet me, and my compassionate stepson, Peter. I had a very difficult recovery, mainly from the loss of my children being gone and missing them so much! I remember many heartbreaking nights missing my kids and trying to cope with all the pain. Peter would bring me ice packs and just be there for me. By this time, my daughter and son were both away in the S.O. I tried calling for two weeks, but the S.O. staff would not allow me to speak with them.

Jeremy was almost sixteen and Jessica was eighteen. Jeremy's sixteenth birthday was coming up and the S.O. promised me that my son could come home for his birthday. Birthdays are very big in my family and we were all going to have a lovely party for my son with his family who loved him.

I finally got through after three weeks of crying because I couldn't reach my son, on top of recovering from my knee with extensive physical therapy. Jeremy told me he could not come home for his birthday; that he was not done with his EPF (Estates Project Force, a boot camp-type training where they fix up buildings and property) and the S.O. would not give approval for him to come home. Jeremy seemed really upset when he called, but he was holding back his emotions.

I knew how important coming home for his big day was to Jeremy, but the S.O. monitored his calls and he was not allowed to show any negative emotions, only positive ones. I was extremely upset and so was all my family.

A month passed and Jessica called to announce, "I'm coming home!" She was not allowed to give me more details until she had gained authorization from the S.O. to do so, another rule I was unaware of at the time. At dinner a couple of months later, Jessica told me what had really happened.

While she was preparing to go to the S.O., the day before she left she was told there was a problem with her fiancé going with her to Flag, the Sea Org in Florida. She and Justin had planned to marry once they both arrived in Florida, but he had an ethics situation and was not approved to go with her. He needed to go to the Mexico S.O. to get this handled before he could join her in Florida.

Earlier, when Jessica and Justin were trying to date before they went into the Sea Org, all I knew about Justin's ethics situation was that the San Francisco Ethics Officer kept a tight rein on him and he was doing conditions for a long time. I guess after about six months they finally could see each other. Jessica was really quiet about what was going on but I did hear that her dad didn't like Justin. I really liked him and after they were back together from routing out of the S.O., he was always welcome and we spent lots of time with both of them. They would go to the lake with us in the summer and we even took him with us to the Mojave Desert for a family dirt biking vacation. The five of us had a fantastic time.

Jessica continued to tell me at dinner that she was devastated about Justin's situation because she was joining the S.O. mainly for him so they could be together. The S.O. promised her that her fiancé would be able to join her soon, but after only two days she could clearly see that he wasn't coming soon and so she wanted to leave and come home.

They were able to talk and Justin decided to leave and go back home, too. They never did get married because the Sea Org separated them from the beginning. The S.O. tried to "handle" Jessica to stay and kept her there for a month against her will, while making her perform menial tasks like washing dishes. She told the people in charge whom she reported to daily that she wanted to come home. Jessica is very feisty and was determined to get out of there. After one month of persistence, she was home and I was so happy and relieved to have her back with me.

She told me that the S.O. in charge yelled at her and would not let her go home until she did her official "route out." She said, "Oh, Mom, please don't tell anyone I said this; I could get in big trouble!" I was beyond furious that they treated her this way and had lied to her about her fiancé joining her. This was all so surreal and shocking to me.

At the seventh-month mark, I still struggled to recover from my surgery but the emotional trauma from missing my son was not helping. I was still on Advil for the pain. In the time that Jeremy was in the S.O., I was only able to speak to him five times. My husband would see me crying because they would not let me talk to him. CR was infuriated and ready to fly me to Florida to get Jeremy, even though my immense knee pain rendered me unable to do so.

During the minimal times Jeremy and I did talk, I could tell something was wrong. He would tell me he was in school and doing well, but then I later learned that Jeremy had sufficient schooling only a handful of times. This was total disregard for the "Power of Attorney for Care of Minor Child" that clearly stated he would attend regular schooling. I didn't believe he was doing well at all. I guess it's a mother's intuition!

The Sea Org had also promised me that Jeremy would continue his orthodontic treatment that he had been having for the past three years and now he was ready for his final stage of treatment—braces. In actuality, he never got any orthodontic treatment. It was another broken promise and the "Power of Attorney for Medical Care of Minor" was also violated.

Jeremy had his driver's permit and needed to continue his hours of driving, another promise the church had ensured me they would handle yet he never had an opportunity to practice while he was there.

Jeremy was in the CMO (Commodore's Messenger Organization), a very high-ranking section in the S.O. because the group had been started by Hubbard to assist him on the Sea Org ship *Apollo*. I learned that for three months Jeremy was in the regular EPF and then went to the CMO EPF. In the seven months he was a member of the Sea Org, he had only a few days off and was paid just thirty dollars a week.

Finally, I got a call from Jeremy that he wanted to come home and that he was going to leave the S.O. I was so excited I was beside myself. Jeremy said it would be a couple of days. The very thought of having him home for Thanksgiving was overwhelmingly thrilling. A few days later, though, he called to say, "I'm still going through the procedure of routing out and I won't be there for Thanksgiving."

Again, I was extremely upset! I called Jeremy on Thanksgiving three times and grew very angry because I couldn't get through. When I finally did reach him, I asked if he was having Thanksgiving dinner.

"No, Mom," he replied. "I am not allowed to be on the S.O. base and around the S.O. members." This was the price of leaving. He was off the base in isolation and under guard. He had to stay away from the members in "good standing." I was really pissed now and so was the rest of the family!

The following week, I called three to four times a day attempting to get my son home. Jeremy was isolated and kept under guard for over a week. He was only sixteen and in isolation? I had to hold it together because this was terrifying me! To a teenager, that must seem like forever. My multiple daily calls went unanswered while he sat in isolation wanting nothing more than to come home. Fortunately, he was finally able to do that!

In leaving the Sea Organization, Jeremy was issued a "freeloader" debt of nine hundred and fifty dollars. Until this debt was paid, he could not take any courses or services with the church. The mind control never stopped.

Chapter Ten

Jeremy and Jessica Back Home

I was ecstatic! I got to the airport early and sat by the gate in anticipation of seeing my son whom I hadn't seen in seven months. Just the thought of hugging him again and not saying goodbye meant the world to me. As he approached, I was flowing with excitement to see him; we hugged and I cried. I kept looking at him, hoping this was not a dream. He had grown so much in the past seven months. Then we went to our favorite place for dinner, Chili's. I asked Jeremy about his seven months in the S.O.

"I don't want to talk about it," he said. "What is important is that I am home now."

I kept trying to find out what he did while there but he adamantly made it clear he did not want to discuss it. I thought this was very strange. Jeremy and I usually talked about everything so this was odd to me. Jeremy seemed tense and uneasy around me. I had no idea at that time what he had really gone through. I was simply full of joy to finally have both of my kids back home.

Although Jessica's stay at home was brief, she and Justin got an apartment together, but changed their mind on rushing into marriage. She was so excited to get her first apartment. We helped her move and my mom and I went over to help her unpack. I really missed her at home but happy for her that she could get her own place.

When Jeremy first got back he seemed introverted and kept things to himself. He didn't seem like the happy boy I used to know. I could tell something was wrong by the way he was acting. At first, he acted a lot older than he was. He was only sixteen. He also seemed nervous just being around me and CR. As time went by and he started working at a motorcycle shop and riding his dirt bike again, as well as making new friends at work, he started being like himself again and seemed more relaxed. Jeremy made payments to the church over a six-month period, to pay what they claimed he owed them, in order to remain in good standing with the church. As a minor legally unable to sign, or be bound to a contract, he paid his "freeloader" debt in full.

I know Jeremy had to give a lot of his check to his S.O. debt and he was doing conditions because of leaving. Jeremy did tell me once or twice when Jessica was going through her mess with her debt that he would never do that. He saw with his own eyes how terrible it was, but Scientology has a way of completely persuading and manipulating one to do what is best for the church. All this was kept secret from me. I would ask questions and Jeremy would say he was handling it with the "proper terminal" (staff person). I was kept in the dark often with my kids when they were working with the Ethics Officer and I couldn't stand it because I felt like my parental rights were totally violated and the dang E.O. was trying to raise my kids. It's awful being a Scientology parent when you don't agree with what Scientology is doing with your kids. The parents who disagree are treated like they are "out-ethics" for not agreeing with the church. Like I said, the mind control never stopped.

Gradually, my son slowly opened up to me. One day he said, "Mom, I know you had a really hard time crying and missing me, but I want you to know it was even harder for me. I cried many nights wanting to come home and I couldn't tell you because the S.O. said I shouldn't tell you while you were recovering from your knee replacement."

He said that being there was really hard on him and that he missed me a lot and was very homesick. I was furious that the church kept this from me. When he was away, I felt his pain—again, a mother's intuition, I guess.

I got Jeremy back in the Scientology school. I tried to get him back in public school, but because he had no official school records for the seven months he was in the S.O., I was having difficulty getting him accepted in public school. After he went back to his Scientology school, the teacher called me in and said Jeremy was really behind and that is when I actually found out that he had had no schooling when he was in the S.O. I had been assured that when he was in the S.O. he would get his proper schooling. When I signed the S.O. contract, it said that he would get his schooling and that was a big thing for me. The Sea Organization had broken their billion-year contract.

Jeremy's teacher even told me that she was surprised how far behind he was and was shocked that he had had very little formal schooling. Per the law,

Jeremy was required to be in school and he only received schooling approximately three days in the seven months he was in the S.O.

A few months later, Jeremy mentioned that his toe was hurting. I asked him about it and he said, "I had an ingrown toenail and had a toe procedure done in the Sea Org by a doctor and it was very painful."

Bob Wright, his assigned guardian, had done nothing to inform me of Jeremy's medical procedure. Bob and I never talked and the same went for his wife. They both violated the S.O. contract I had to sign giving them guardianship, but I was to be informed of any medical concerns. Another violation by Scientology's largest organization.

Jeremy mentioned to CR that the nice shoes that my husband gave him to take to the S.O. were stolen and that he had to wear shoes that were too small, which probably led to him having the painful toe. My husband was shocked that someone in the S.O. would steal Jeremy's shoes. When CR mentioned this to me, I couldn't believe what I was hearing. Kids in the S.O. steal from one another? I thought the S.O. was supposed to be the most ethical place on the planet.

I told Jeremy that as his mom, I should have been told about this. He seemed upset about this procedure, but he was quite reluctant to divulge any information regarding it. His toe continued to hurt and when I asked Jeremy if he wanted to go to the doctor he said "No!" This put up another red flag for me. I had an uneasy feeling about this "toe procedure." The way Jeremy didn't really want to talk about it or anything about his time in the S.O. made me wonder if there was more to it.

Well, there was. Something happened while Jeremy was on S.O. staff that was far worse than keeping quiet about troubles he was having. I found out they made him sign a gag order about something. He was told that if he would keep quiet there would be no problem, but if he ever spoke up, he would have to pay Scientology three million dollars! Did I mention that Jeremy was only sixteen years old when he signed the contract?

Chapter Eleven

The Three-Million-Dollar Gag Contract

Six months later, we went to Clear Lake for Mom's 4th of July birthday week. I was so happy to have our tradition back as a family celebrating her birthday. While I was out floating on an air mattress getting some sun rays, Jeremy was talking to his grandma. Mom was asking Jeremy about his stay in the S.O.

He slipped and said, "Oh Nonie, I am not allowed to talk about that. I signed a three-million-dollar contract to never talk about what occurred when I was there and if I do talk about it, I will have to pay the Church of Scientology three million dollars and lose my eternity!"

He added that if he were to break this contract, he would no longer be able to take any Scientology courses. Thus, "lose his eternity." Scientologists thought that they were doomed as spiritual beings, you see, if they didn't get all the way up "the Bridge."

My mom said, "What?! That is not legal or binding, Jeremy! You were only sixteen years old."

She asked if he received a copy of the order he signed, and he said no. Mom shared with me what Jeremy just told her and I was beyond upset! I tried to talk about it with Jeremy and he was upset too and wouldn't talk to me. I talked more with my mom and neither of us could come up with any answers regarding what really happened to Jeremy.

Mom and I were still in Scientology at this point. She was an Operating Thetan (OT) 5. She was an opinion leader among Scientologists in the Bay

Area. Everyone loved my mom and she was highly looked up to. She was very unhappy with the whole situation with both my kids just like I had been.

Earlier, before we even knew about the gag contract, what had already happened with my kids was waking both my mom and me up about Scientology. Mom tried hard to help me and we both wrote up many Knowledge Reports on what went on with Jessica and Jeremy. Knowledge Reports are reports a scientologist writes up to the appropriate Scientology person like an Ethics Officer if she or he feels something is wrong and needs help. Scientology never did anything about the KRs we wrote up and sent in. I bet they just tossed them.

We couldn't fathom any reason why a "church" would order anyone, much less a teenager, to sign a contract blackmailing them into silence. What could have taken place that was so damning and horrible that they required a Three-Million-Dollar gag contract? Finding out this news from my son was the straw that broke the camel's back for me. I was done with Scientology and all their lies and controlling acts with my children. Mom felt the same way. The next step was to do something about it. In our case, we'd had it, and we were going to let the so-called Church of Scientology know we were sick of their evil ways.

Chapter Twelve

Resigning from Scientology: Disconnection Begins

Effective August 30, 2010, my mom and I resigned from the Church of Scientology. Neither of us could deny that we were obviously a part of a corrupt and manipulating organization and we no longer wanted any part of it. We each wrote a resignation letter to Scientology and put it in the mail. We stated in our letters that we were resigning from the Church of Scientology as of August 30, 2010 and we did not want to be a part of Scientology anymore. We made it short and to the point.

On August 30, 2010, the day we resigned, Mom and I met my kids at our office to explain to them that we had resigned and why. We spent several hours discussing it with them. Jessica got very upset. She voiced her concerns that her grandmother and I would be declared Suppressive and if she kept in contact with us, then she would be declared Suppressive as well. She also was very worried about her father and what he might do. She said, "Daddy is going to be really upset!"

Jessica also expressed that she and Jeremy would never disconnect from us but then they would have to disconnect from their dad.

I said, "No, you don't! Wait a minute! We are not telling you to disconnect from anyone. We just do not want to do Scientology and we are fine that you both continue with it."

Jessica looked so worried. Jeremy, on the other hand, was more receptive and agreed with a lot of things we were saying. We told him and his sister to take a couple of days to think about what we said; to digest it before they told their father.

The next weekend was Labor Day and I was told by a friend that Jim told Jessica and Jeremy, "If you don't disconnect from your mom, then I will disconnect from you, because no one is going to take my eternity away from me!"

My friend Mari called me and said that she had heard that eternity declaration directly from Jim. He told Mari that he had said that to our kids, and although they never told me that he said that, I did believe it. Jim was always a true believer, die-hard Scientologist, and he definitely believed Scientology was his path to eternity. I never believed in Scientology to that extent. I would rather be at the lake with my kids and husband having fun.

We were all up at the lake for Labor Day, a big family weekend for us, and my daughter was very upset with me for resigning. Jeremy was a little more understanding. I noticed Jessica spent most of the weekend on the phone and limited her time with us. I was really distraught all weekend because it had been only one week since I resigned and I was already threatened with losing my kids according to what Jim told Mari. I still couldn't fathom his motives and why he would force our kids to make a "Sophie's Choice" between their mom or their dad?

After my mom and I resigned, Pat Wehner, the Mission Holder, and Mary Jo Hyland, my mom's friend, came over to our workplace to talk to my mom and try to "handle" her—meaning, convince her not to resign. Pat told my mom, "This will be a shock wave across the planet!"

Mom said clearly, "Lori and I are done."

They both looked sick about this and left. In the following weeks, Mary Jo attempted to try to handle my mom and coerce her not to resign from the COS and not to request a repayment of her unused money on account.

Why a "shock wave across the planet"? That was because my mom was such a big opinion leader and had been a fantastic Field Staff Member (FSM), getting a lot of people into Scientology and "up the Bridge." Many Scientologists looked up to my mom because of her FSM skills as well as her nutrition business. Mom had many Scientology nutrition clients. In contrast, I didn't have very many Scientology clients. Mom got so many people on the Bridge that Pat knew if he lost her it would be highly detrimental financially to his mission. My mom had also been on staff at his mission, but she took a break after the whole mess with my kids.

The mission people continued to try very hard to get her back. Mary Jo tried to show her the Scientology policies and tell her the consequences of leaving and getting her money back. I think they thought if they got my mom to come back then she would get me to follow. Wrong! Mom and I stayed firm on our decision to leave. My children were very upset with me and they would not listen to why I stayed firm on my decision. I was extremely upset about possibly losing my children and what I had gone through the past five years with my kids. I couldn't believe that Scientologists were willing to rip apart my family, particularly via people we had known and interacted with for a long time.

Looking back to when we were still in Scientology, Mom had joined staff like I did back in 1978. She fulfilled a two-and-a-half year contract at the Stevens Creek Mission in Santa Clara then she was on course off and on and did her OT levels up to OT 5. She helped out as FSM at Kurt Wilson and Tom Chandler's field group for several years after her staff contract. Then for several years she wasn't doing much. She got pressured by Scientology Flag registrars to do her L-11 (touted as something that would turn you into a Super-Thetan of sorts) and some other auditing at Flag in Clearwater, Florida.

When I was working at the Scientology school, I had to be on course so I signed up at the San Jose Mission where John Allender was the Mission Holder, but I didn't have to deal with him because Pat Wehner was my supervisor. I liked Pat and felt comfortable at the mission. I got Mom to come down and check it out and many of her old staff people were there and she liked them. They recruited her for staff and she signed up at the San Jose Mission. Pat Wehner was the Mission Holder by then and she liked Pat a lot. She was on staff when I had to do my first knee replacement in 2008 and she took time off to help me. During my second knee replacement and the heavy recruiting of both my kids for the S.O., my mom took a break and didn't go back because she was trying to help me.

We had each decided to write a resignation letter, and we were thankful to my stepdad, Val. He encouraged us both to take a stand and write the letters. He said not many people do that and he thought my kids would respect us more, rather than just wait until we were declared Suppressive Persons because we were no longer doing Scientology "services." Mom and I felt more "at cause" (a Scientology term meaning effective) by resigning because we wanted Scientology to know that we were totally done with them and wanted nothing else to do with the so-called religion. What they had done to my kids, my mom's grandchildren, was beyond gross and we both wanted no part of what we now perceived to be a heartless organization.

We never regretted writing our resignation letters and were proud of ourselves for having the integrity to do so. I think it takes a lot of courage to write a resignation letter and I feel that was the start of my freedom and my strength to fight this fight for my kids and end the disconnection practices of Scientology that had upset or ruined so many families and relationships.

After we had resigned, I was not doing well because my kids were being distant and I was so worried I was going to lose them to disconnection. I also struggled, trying to sort out my feelings, trying to figure out for myself if I could salvage what I did find helpful about Scientology. I found Marty Rathbun, a former high-ranking member of the COS, who counseled other ex–members to help them with their betrayals from Scientology and assist them if they chose to continue Scientology counseling. I wanted help with my kids and to do what I could to prevent separation from them by the Scientology Disconnection Policy.

I visited Marty in December 2010. He was in Texas and I had not told anyone of my whereabouts or what I was doing. The COS strongly opposes any of their members (or ex-members) who choose to practice Scientology outside the church. They refer to it as "squirreling." I explained my situation with my children and all the abuses Scientology had visited upon my children and our family. Marty had been a member of the Sea Organization, working directly under David Miscavige, who began running Scientology after Hubbard died. Marty really helped me. He advised me to continue to try to talk to my kids and to try to see them.

After arriving home, the day after my visit with Marty in Texas, I was harassed and threatened by John Allender, now an undercover operative for the Church of Scientology. That morning, while I was at work a woman called and asked what our business hours were. I told her and she hung up quickly. I thought that was odd. I finished my workday and said goodbye to my mom. As I was walking to my car, I noticed John Allender. He approached me in the parking lot in an aggressive manner and asked this horrific question: "Do you enjoy beatings?"

Suddenly, I felt terrified by him. Apparently, he had been aware of my whereabouts all along. This became obvious when he added, "You've been doing some squirreling over the weekend."

My heart was racing and I turned and ran the best I could with a knee replacement back into my office. I flew into my mom's office looking as white as a ghost. I could barely get my thoughts together to explain what had just happened. She was alarmed and, of course, immediately worried about me. I reported this incident to the police. It became rather clear to me that I was being followed. I decided to share my short story on Marty Rathbun's blog, "Moving on up a Little Higher" and I went public about John Allender's threats. This was the first time I wrote anything publicly. I thought, *Enough is enough!* What kind of "church" did I used to belong to? It was frightening, to say the least.

Before my children officially disconnected from me and my mom, I found out through a friend that my son was hesitant about disconnecting. I heard that Rick Melrose, an OT 8 highest level of Scientology and the chaplain at San Jose Mission, had asked to see my son. He told Jeremy that he had had many mothers in his lifetimes and that I was just his mother *this* lifetime and he should not lose his eternity over me. I feel this persuaded and manipulated my son to finally disconnect from me. This insane sales pitch was despicable! I had known Rick for a long time and considered him a friend. How could he do this? He actually assisted in breaking up my family!

Jeremy and Jessica were coerced and manipulated by Scientology and their father to disconnect from me because I had left the "church" and "squirreled" and gone public about John Allender's threat to me. I resigned because of what Scientology did to my children, I "squirreled" because I saw Marty to help me get my family back together, and I went public because a Scientologist threatened me. I think most people understand my actions.

Shortly after this, I spoke to Pat Wehner to request a refund of the $11,000 I had on account for future services. I was shocked when my daughter met with my mom and me and told us that if we asked for our money back, I would become an enemy to her and to the church. I was also told that Pat had already spent my money, and that he would have to pay it back out of his own pocket; that I shouldn't have gone public about the threats made against me by John Allender. Jessica didn't seem to care that I had actually been threatened.

I told her that I wanted my money back, I would not be returning for any services, and I had every intention of going public with details about the injustices that Scientology had inflicted upon me, my family, and my children!

I tried to explain to Jessica that I just wanted to be her mom. Because I left Scientology did not mean we couldn't be mother and daughter anymore. She disagreed. She said that I couldn't be her mom if I didn't go back and get in good standing with Scientology. I couldn't believe this. It was so heartbreaking to hear her say this to me. She got up and left. I just sat there in shock!

My children both told me that unless I got back in good standing with Scientology and do the A-E steps to rectify the situation, they could not be around me. This is the Disconnection Policy: HANDLE OR DISCONNECT! Unfortunately, my children were strongly influenced to disconnect from me because even for the love of my children, I cannot be emotionally blackmailed by Scientology to do these steps.

The A-E steps are steps on how to get back in good standing with Scientology if one has been declared a Suppressive Person. Being critical of Scientology, being anti-Scientology, speaking out publicly about Scientology, are just a few of the various reasons one can be declared a Suppressive Person by Scientology. In my case, I simply resigned from Scientology and just one week later was threatened with Scientology disconnection, which meant I would lose my only two children.

After four months had passed, I went to see a former Scientologist to help me because my kids were pulling away from me. The following day, I got threatened again in the parking lot at work by a Scientologist who also was a big influence on my kids to disconnect from me. I spoke out publicly about this man threatening me and the injustices that Scientology had inflicted on my children and me. I got declared a Suppressive Person for that, although Scientology never called me in directly to tell me that. I just heard from a few of my friends that I was declared.

I have tried reaching out to my kids in person, through text and email, via friends and family, and lastly tried to work directly with the International Justice Chief (IJC) of Scientology, who I was told is the only person in Scientology I can talk to. Nothing worked, and supposedly nothing will unless I do these gruesome A-E steps.

It's too long to go over all the steps, but I will explain a few of them from what I understand them to be. I would have to stop speaking out about my disconnection with my kids and just shut my mouth. Then, make a public announcement that my actions for speaking out were ignorant and not based on facts. I would have to retrain on all Scientology courses I had previously done at my expense. Another step would be to do a long and arduous amends project for Scientology and only the IJC can approve when they feel I've done enough.

I can't do these A-E steps because I'm not lying about what happened to my children and me. Scientology destroyed my family and how in the world could I do an amends project for that. I think what needs to happen is that Scientology apologizes to me and gives me my family back! I also never want to be a Scientologist again so why would I want to retrain everything. As I've said countless times before, I just want to be Jessica and Jeremy's mom. That's all I've ever wanted and if Scientology had not taken my sweet children from me then we wouldn't be in this awful, inhumane situation. No religion or group should ever break up a family.

I hope my children can read what the A-E steps really are because my son once told me that I could do the A-E steps and not be a Scientologist. He doesn't understand that yes, I would have to go back to being a Scientologist to do these steps.

I'm clearly seeing now the strong signs of my kids disconnecting from me. On February 1, 2011, I received this text message from my daughter: "Ok. Honestly, I don't feel comfortable going to you and CR's birthday dinner and sitting there acting like nothing is wrong when I am very enturbulated [upset] about what is happening. I do wish you and CR a very happy birthday, but I'm not going to come on Saturday. I will be there for Papa's on Sunday to wish him a happy birthday and see the family."

Since my mom and I could not be "HANDLED," my children were manipulated and forced to disconnect from us as of February 6, 2011. I remember that day very clearly. I'm not certain who manipulated Jessica, but when she sent me texts and my only terminal was the International Justice Chief, I clearly knew someone was telling her that as she probably didn't even know the IJC existed before that.

Like I said earlier, I do know who it was who finally got to Jeremy and swayed him to disconnect from me. It was Rick Melrose. He was a man I had known for a long time. I knew him when I was a teenager at the Stevens Creek Mission. He was one of the lecturers for new Scientologists. I saw him later back in the middle Nineties. He was the Chaplain for the San Jose Mission where I was doing services. He even was a Chaplain for me and CR regarding some issues we were having; Rick made things worse. CR and I didn't like talking with him, so we worked things out on our own. Then after I resigned, Pat, the Mission Holder, had Jeremy come in and talk to Rick. This person I thought was a friend revealed himself to be a cold Scientologist who persuaded my son to not see me anymore.

February 6th was my dad's birthday and my birthday is February 8th. We were all meeting for dinner to celebrate on February 6, 2011. I was really nervous when my husband and I arrived. We got there early. Everyone was there except my kids. They arrived shortly after and pretty much ignored me. They sat at the opposite side of our large table. It was the most uncomfortable family get-together ever. My kids were shunning me in front of the family. When everyone was about to leave, my son hugged me, but not my daughter. That was it, and the saddest day because it was the first day my kids cut all ties with me. It was heartbreaking, to say the least.

Also that February, my half-sister was pregnant and Jeremy and Jessica could not be there to revel in the joy of seeing their new baby cousin and become a part of his life. My half-sister and half-brother were raised Catholic and never were Scientologists. My dad and stepmom were never Scientologists, either. They couldn't understand this whole disconnection thing and why Jeremy and Jessica were now distant from our family.

Also in my family is my stepdad, Val, and he is not a Scientologist. Val has two daughters. Mom introduced them both to Scientology and only one became a Scientologist. When Mom and I left Scientology, my Scientology stepsister also disconnected from us.

So the only Scientologists in my family were my kids and my stepsister.

My kids ended up disconnecting from my whole family, including the non-Scientologists. They also disconnected from all our friends that were still in contact with me or my mom. My kids' Facebook pages are monitored by the Scientology Facebook police and they make sure my kids are not in touch with any of my family or our mutual friends. They watch my kids like hawks and to this day they have Scientologists keeping an eye on all their social media accounts.

My kids were very close with all the family members I mentioned and I know they were heartbroken not to have their family around anymore. This is how Scientology destroyed my family. The non-Scientologists did not understand this cruelty that Scientology enforces in breaking up families. My cousin was very close with Jessica, but Jessica had to disconnect from her, too, because my cousin stays in touch with me. Anyone can clearly see that by making my kids shut everyone out, they will have no chance to hear any criticism about Scientology. This is how Scientology keeps their members controlled.

It is so wrong that Scientology has the power to break up families and, in my opinion, that makes Scientology one of the most despicable organizations on Earth.

Chapter Thirteen

Taking My Ex, Jim, to Court, the FBI and the Squirrel-Busters

My ex, Jim, owed back child support. When I was still in Scientology, Jim was often behind on his child support payments. There were two times I remember he went away to Florida to do Scientology services, but did not pay his child support. I could not go outside the Scientology Organization for help, because when you're in Scientology that is forbidden. I had to handle it internally. I wrote up many reports to the Scientology Ethics Officer for help on getting my past owed child support. The reports did not help especially when he went to Florida. I couldn't believe they would even let Jim go to Florida for services when his child support was owed.

I knew that after the disconnection I would never see my past-owed child support because Jim and Scientology labeled me a Suppressive Person, which meant to them I was as evil as Hitler because I left Scientology and didn't agree with what they wanted to do with my kids. So I decided I had better use the court system to help me get my child support and hopefully the courts would help me get my son back from the Scientology disconnection.

Jim had broken the custody agreement. When we got divorced, the agreement was I would have the kids sixty percent and he would have them forty percent. So I started all the paperwork to get dates for the court hearing. Then I found out during my second visit to Marty's that Jim had hired an attorney, most likely a Scientologist, who would stall the court case until Jeremy was eighteen, so I couldn't bring the Scientology disconnection up in court. It was bad PR for the church but also a normal type of obfuscation of law. They didn't care.

Also during this time, I began working with the FBI about my son's time spent in the Sea Org. The FBI was investigating a case on Human Trafficking in the Sea Org. I gave them all the information I had and they even came to my office to interview both my mom and me. The same day they interviewed me they went to see if they could interview my son at a job site where he was helping his dad on a construction project, but he was not there. They went a few different times that day and no sign of my son or his dad.

I told my FBI agent that Scientology might have a way of tracking people who try to help me with my disconnection situation and I alerted them that Scientology might find out if they are going to see him. My guess is Scientology found out somehow and made sure Jeremy and Jim were not at work.

The FBI also interviewed one of my lifelong friends who had been a witness in Jeremy's recruiting for the Sea Org. After my agent interviewed my mom and me, she wanted me to keep her updated on my situation and report to her any harassment I experienced from Scientology.

I was so torn up over losing my children to Scientology disconnection that I needed to go back to Texas to get help from Marty. I was mentally unable to handle the pain from the disconnection and the abuses I received from the "church." In April 2011, I went back to Marty's place. I told only my family that I was going because I didn't want Scientology to harass me again.

The evening I arrived, Marty, his wife Monique (whom he called "Mosey"), and I were taking a walk and both Mosey and I sensed that someone was following us. We saw a few vans driving around, but they were keeping their distance. I told Marty I was a little nervous because of my last harassment with John Allender back in December when Allender threatened me in my parking lot at work. Marty reassured us that he didn't think anyone was following us. That evening, Marty told us that he was going to go out to his truck and get his video camera; that he hadn't used it in a month and thought he should charge it. He put the camera inside by the front door to charge. I thought that was a little odd that he told me that. Maybe he had a gut instinct that he might need his camera.

The following day, April 18, 2011, was my first day in counseling with Marty. Before we started our counseling that morning, Marty told me that the plumber was going to stop by and that he had a really loud, obnoxious knock on the door. I thought to myself, *Marty just wants to give me a heads up*. We started our counseling and I mainly wanted to discuss my grief over losing my kids and the scary encounter I had had four months prior with John Allender. We took a break for lunch around noon.

You would never guess who showed up. John Allender, the man who had threatened me in December, and Mark Warlick, the Director of Special Affairs of Los Gatos Org, where my kids were recruited, both had followed me from San Jose to Texas to try to, I assume, stop me from meeting with Marty. They arrived with two other men in light blue T-shirts with Marty's picture on the front that said "Squirrel." They had cameras taped to their heads and a cameraman. They slammed on Marty's door while I was downstairs having a lunch break, similar to the way the recruiters slammed on my door when they were recruiting my son for the Sea Org. I thought to myself, *Wow, Marty was right about the plumber being so loud.* The loud knocking went on for a bit so I looked out the window from downstairs and saw it was John Allender. I was terrified.

Marty told me to lock my door and stay inside. Then Marty called the sheriff and we reported the harassment and the stalking. I also reported this to the FBI agent that I was already working with. When I called my agent, she answered right away and I updated her on what was going on. She told me to call the local authorities and immediately get a police report to send to her. Marty said he would take care of it and he filed a police report for us.

That afternoon, Marty said he had some high-ranking former Scientologist there to visit and I was just this mom trying to get help with her disconnected kids. In other words, he found it strange that Scientology was putting so much heat on me. To have those goons show up meant there was something going on that was odd. He asked me what it was that I knew or that Scientology thought I knew that they were so worried about. I told Marty the only big thing that came to mind was the three-million-dollar gag contract that Scientology had threatened my son with.

Marty thought that maybe that was it, but the question was, why did they threaten Jeremy with an amount so large? Three million? He was just a kid. This is when we really started thinking more about that gag order. Was it the connection with his Uncle Bob Wright? Was it something Jeremy saw or heard? We continued to discuss it and didn't come up with a good explanation.

This incident left me clearly shaken and even more determined to stop these abuses from occurring. Three days later, a van with the logo Squirrel Busters on the side drove down the street near Marty's house so we started filming them and when they saw us filming they drove away.

Then one morning I saw a man watching Mosey, Marty and me from across the canal near Marty's house while we were outside having our morning coffee. I stayed for two weeks and I would ride Mosey's bicycle around the neighborhood for exercise and often noticed vehicles following me at a distance.

Also on April 18th, the same day that the Squirrel Busters showed up, my husband called me from San Jose and said that I had received a letter mailed to our San Jose home address from an attorney. He opened it for me and the letter was a court action against me, serving me at my home address, requiring me to answer it in San Jose within a week. That meant I would have had to jump on a plane and come right home. We figured Jim Leake probably hired an attorney that Scientology wanted him to get so that I would have to cut my Texas trip short. That's how badly Scientology wanted me to stay away from Marty so he couldn't hear my whole story.

Thankfully, I hired an attorney while I was in Texas and was able to stay there the whole two weeks. I handled everything with my attorney from Texas. I found out Jim did have an attorney and yes, he was always struggling with money so I had no idea how he paid for that. Maybe Scientology was involved; not sure though.

Another weird thing that happened was that the FBI wanted my police report that Marty and I made on John Allender and Mark Warlick and the other two Squirrel Busters. The police report was incorrect and did not state all the facts. The report got switched around and said more about Marty's taking the Squirrel Busters' microphone than it did about what the aggressive Scientologists had done.

Marty and I had to talk more with the police, and the District Attorney of the City of Corpus Christi personally came over to see me at Marty's house and apologized for the mix-up. He said he would get me a proper report with the right facts. The D.A. also apologized for what had happened to me under his jurisdiction. I called the FBI and said I was working on getting the correct police report and would get it to them as soon as I got my copy.

I never got a copy, though. The whole thing was bizarre. I told the FBI I never got one and they took over from there. I never heard anything else about it.

During the time I was in Texas, my father, stepmother, and brother tried to talk to my children on Easter to get them to look at what Scientology was doing to me. I told my parents it's called "Fair Game." Fair game is a cruel strategy Scientology enacts on those who are blowing the whistle on the abuses of Scientology. It means they are going to do whatever it takes to punish and harass the critic using any and all means possible. Although Hubbard had declared the policy defunct years before, it was common knowledge the church still applied it secretly. Basically, "anything goes" to harm anti-Scientologists.

My kids refused to look at anything critical of their church. There was a video that Marty captured of the Squirrel Busters when they had first arrived at Marty's house and that was the same day Allender and Warlick followed me across state lines. My parents were trying to get Jeremy and Jessica to watch it. They refused and my son started crying because they said they couldn't talk about it and that they needed to leave. My daughter was also really upset. That was it, end of discussion, they had to leave. My parents couldn't believe how their grandkids were acting. They couldn't understand why they would not even look at this video of these men following me to Texas and harassing me. Also, my parents were aware that my kids knew the main Squirrel Buster, John Allender, and that they knew about the time he had threatened me in the parking lot at work. Why wouldn't they want to see the video? Made no sense to my parents!

When I was in Scientology, I had no idea how Scientology fair-gamed people and all the abuses they committed on critics. I really was in the dark; that's why I was so shocked when all this fair game was happening to me. I kind of knew about disconnection when people spoke out, but I don't remember where I learned that. Maybe it was from when my coworker at the Scientology school was crying about her daughter being recruited for the Sea Org and she told me there was nothing she could do to stop it.

Shortly after this, my children were no longer allowed to be around any member of the family that was critical of Scientology or anyone who had tried to get my children to see how cruel this "church" was, and that disconnecting from family and those who love you most is immoral and wrong. It was all horrific. My parents were in their seventies and could not be a part of their grandchildren's lives because of this disconnection policy.

When I got back home from visiting Marty, I sent my daughter a text telling her I loved her and to please look at both sides. I told her about being followed by John Allender and Mark Warlick and to please watch the Squirrel Buster video.

On May 1, 2011, I received this text from Jessica about looking at both sides:

"I did. I even watched that video. I am a Scientologist and I expect that to be respected. I told you before that this would be a complete different story if u just decided not to be a part of the church anymore and went off and did ur own thing. But u are attacking my group. U are being part of a squirrel group. By definition and fact they are squirrels and are trying to put a bad name to my church.

"And I don't see how we can have a comm line when u r attacking my group and committing suppressive acts and by definition in the ethics book u r committing

suppressive acts and that is lrh. I really don't want things to be like this and I'd like to handle it but we can't have an OK comm line until this stops. Scientology and my friends that are Scientologists have helped me majorly in life.

"I believe in it 100% and that won't change. This has even been a wake up call for me and made me realize how important it really is for me to get up my bridge now."

Jessica had told me she was talking to John Allender, so I'm sure he was a big part of the coaching, along with her dad. John and Jim were friends. I also know Pat Wehner worked with John and they were big buds, so I think there was definitely more than one Scientologist coaching and manipulating my kids to disconnect from me. Also, my ex always called Bob Wright for advice. I think the coaches were John Allender, Rick Melrose, Bob Wright (Jim's brother who worked directly under Miscavige), Pat Wehner, Mark Warlick, and Lynda Allender. These were all opinion leaders to my kids and they were manipulating and controlling Jessica and Jeremy.

A few days after I got back home, I found sexual libel about me on the Internet. It was a "blog" written by a person calling itself "Minerva," while pretending to be Marty Rathbun. It even used his name for the website when it wasn't his. In addition to Minerva's slander, a commenter on the blog used my name to continue to perpetuate the lies.

This "Dear Diary" article had very personal things probably taken from my "confidential" counseling folders and put on the Internet for the world to see. It was cruel, sick, and another "fair game" tactic Scientology uses on ex-members for leaving and speaking up. In this Dear Diary article, they made reference to my limp from my smaller leg and my breast enhancement, which was private stuff. I reported the Dear Diary article to my FBI agent and it went in my file. Later on, we found out that Scientology admitted they were responsible for that website.

At Easter, my mom and I sent Jessica and Jeremy Easter cards with money and they both sent them back, saying they could not accept them because we were not in good standing with their church. It broke our hearts that they returned them.

On Mother's Day, I invited both of my kids over for a barbecue. They told me they could not see me. I spent a very sorrowful day, the first Mother's Day without my children. My mom and I had an awfully sad time.

On May 27, 2011, I found a package in my mailbox with no stamp and no return address, which implied that someone had physically placed it in my mailbox—a federal crime. Included were some pamphlets and a letter that read:

"It has come to our attention that Marty Rathbun is auditing PCs who are smoking dope. Perhaps you are not fully aware of the effects drugs can have on an individual. Therefore, I am sending you the Truth about Drugs booklets, which are very educational on the dangerous effects of drugs. Minerva."

Minerva, the troll, who wrote the sexual libel Dear Diary article about me. They were trying hard to mess with my head and were insinuating that I was smoking dope, which I was not. But it was all too typical of Scientology.

Jeremy turned eighteen in June and I could not share this very special day with my son. I asked him if we could do something fun together for his birthday and I got no response. It was another birthday we missed together because of Scientology!

None of this broke me. It only motivated me to be more resolute and fight even harder to get my kids back. That's the mistake Scientology has made with its perceived enemies for decades.

Chapter Fourteen

Taking the Fight to Scientology

A good thing happened in June that year. I had contacted Jim's sister and sister-in-law. Jim never told them about the disconnection with my kids and how my kids were torn apart from their mother and family. They couldn't believe what had happened when I revealed the truth. I shared my story and they both felt really bad. They wanted to help with reuniting me with my kids. I asked them not to tell Jim or he would make them disconnect from me. I shared everything with them. We were planning a reunion with my kids once we were all back together again.

I had found out some big news from a Scientology friend who was secretly talking to me. Secretly, because if they got caught talking to me, they would be kicked out of Scientology and declared a Suppressive Person like I had been.

My friend is still involved and under the radar as of this writing, not wanting to lose a family member who is definitely in. I have another friend still in good standing, but they are at the same point and do not want to lose a family member. I get data from these two people and I don't want to say who they are.

The first person I mentioned told me that Jeremy's uncle, Jim's brother, Bob Wright, who was also Jeremy's guardian in the S.O., had left the Sea Organization after several decades of being in it. The person did not know if Bob had "blown" (escaped without properly routing out of the organization) or if he left in good standing. I called Jim's sister and told her about her brother Bob leaving. She had already heard and told me he was coming to visit her. I advised her that if Bob got paid off, not to talk to him about me because he would most likely be monitored. When he came to visit, I told her to look for any cars parked outside that seemed suspicious, and to let me know if he had to take sudden calls. She called me after he had left and said yes to both things; that there was a black car outside her gate that was parked during Bob's stay and that he got sudden calls.

I then told her that I had a mutual friend with Bob named Tom DeVocht. Bob took over Tom's position working under David Miscavige in the S.O. when Tom left. Bob and Tom were good friends. I also told her that I had asked Tom if he could go visit Bob to see if he blew or left in good standing. I had recently found Bob's address, and Bob lived only an hour away from Tom. Tom said sure. He wanted to see if Bob was okay and if he needed anything. Tom and I decided he would wait a bit before he would go to see Bob.

In July 2011, my mom turned seventy-two and we had a family celebration at the lake. My two children always celebrated this fun week at the lake with us. Jessica and Jeremy were across the lake with my cousin at her place, but did not come over to see us. My kids did go over to my dad's house to get their life jackets and they barely stayed a few minutes. I was told they both acted strangely with my parents, sister, and brother-in-law. For my parents, this was heartbreaking. When they told me how the kids had acted, I wept in my dad's arms.

That evening, Jeremy sent me another disconnection text that read:

"Mom, I'm having a very hard time too and I never thought in my right mind that this would happen to us and it is a big bummer. But you know what you and Nonie need to do to put this family back together and that's that. I really hope you guys fix this and we are all a family again. I miss you very much and hope everything is better soon, but I can't be around you guys with this going on. You are my mother I will love you and miss you too."

What Jeremy was talking about when he said I know what I need to do to fix this is the A-E steps, which I described earlier.

We were so very sad that year spending Mom's birthday week without our Jessica and Jeremy. During the week, the court case happened with my ex regarding past owed child support and the disconnection. Since my ex's attorney stalled the case till after Jeremy turned eighteen, I could not get help by the courts regarding the broken custody agreement with the disconnection and not being able to see my son. I did, however, get my past owed child support.

On July 15, 2011, I received this text from Jeremy:

"Mom...Please just handle this situation. You know what steps you need to do. It's that easy and if me and sissy aren't worth doing that then I have nothing else to say. I do love and miss you but I can't be around you with this going on."

I don't think Jeremy knows what the A-E steps really are. He was probably told the steps are easy to do and your mom must not love you if she won't do them. I'm almost certain my kids were told a lot of lies about me.

In July, my son changed his phone number so I could no longer text him.

Scientology was manipulating my kids again to believe that I had lied about everything. If I went along with what Scientology supposedly wanted, I would have to make a public announcement that I had lied. I would have to pay tens of thousands of dollars for Scientology security check "counseling" and do hundreds of hours of amends for something I had told the truth about. For the love of my children, I could never go back to Scientology, not after what I'd experienced with the abuses committed.

Jessica turned twenty-one in August 2011 and I sent her balloons and a beautiful card to her place of employment. I got no response. I also asked her if we could do something special for her big day and not tell anyone so we could be together. No response. I was crushed not being able to be with my daughter on her special birthday.

My sister was pregnant and had just had a beautiful baby shower to which Jessica had been invited. No response. My sister was not even a Scientologist, but because she was connected to me, Scientology most likely made her cut ties.

The summer of 2011 was my first summer without my kids since they were born. It was such an unhappy summer for all of us cut off from Jessica and Jeremy. We all missed them very much and hoped they would come back soon to their loving family who cared so much for them.

In August, my Facebook page was hacked three times from Texas and twice from Washington. I reported it to the authorities. I turned it into the FBI. The hacking stopped for a while after I reported it to Facebook.

The hacking started up again and it would say on my device that someone logged in from another place. I took snapshots and turned over to the FBI and Facebook where they had logged in. I also took the evidence to the Lakeport Police Department.

Another thing happened in August, the San Jose Mission moved half a block away from the office where I worked with my mom. How ironic that Jim had Jeremy working construction there, so my son was working half a block away from me and yet I couldn't see him.

I kept trying to get my money back from the San Jose Mission that I had on account, which was never used for services. Pat Wehner would not give it back unless I signed a "Claims and Verification" form signing away my rights, and did the steps and "conditions" in Scientology that were required by them.

Their form stated that I couldn't go to an outside third party for redress of grievances. This would have violated my constitutional rights.

I decided not to go to Small Claims Court regarding the $12,000 I was owed. My stepdad, the attorney, said that Scientology would settle, but I thought that if I did that it would make it worse for me and my kids. Also, my mom got her money back and had to sign church documents that stated she could not speak out. She got $25,000 back; that is why she didn't speak out afterward. I didn't want my money back if I had to sign those Scientology forms, and not be able to speak out about how Scientology took my kids from me. That is why I chose not to get my money back.

In September 2011, I did my first interview with Mark Bunker for his upcoming movie *Knowledge Report*. On the video, I discussed the disconnection with my kids. I had a difficult time doing the interview because it was so emotional for me.

On October 9, 2011, my friend Tom decided to go see Bob Wright. Tom and I kept this meeting private and we didn't discuss the exact date until the day before. I told Tom I was worried he would get followed because of what happened with my own experiences. I also mentioned to Tom that Bob was Jeremy's guardian in the S.O. during the time Scientology made Jeremy sign that three-million-dollar gag contract. I said Bob might know what that whole thing was about.

Tom assured me that Scientology was not bothering him right then or following him. "Everything will be fine," he said. Tom called me to tell me he was on his way. I said okay and to keep me posted. Then, as Tom was twenty minutes or so into his drive to see Bob he called me and told me he noticed cars following him. When he got to Bob's place, he noticed another car parked nearby with people inside. I reminded him I had been worried about that. When he got closer, he saw Bob pull quickly out of the driveway in a black SUV and take off. Tom pulled up to the house and parked. He saw Bob's wife in the window. Tom was good friends with her as well. Then he noticed that she closed all the blinds and turned the security lights on. Tom knocked on the door but she would not answer. He waited a bit and left a nice note for Bob, saying that he stopped by to say hi and asked if Bob needed anything.

Then Tom left and called me. He couldn't believe what had just happened and how Scientology somehow had found out he was going there. They must have intercepted our phone calls. He also couldn't believe he was followed. Later, I learned that Mike Rinder accompanied Tom so he would have a witness.

I did hear from some ex-Scientologists that Bob got paid off by Scientology, but I had no real proof. That could be another reason why Tom was followed. Having been David Miscavige's right-hand guy, he was very familiar with Scientology dirty tricks. When I talked to Mike Rinder about all of this on a later trip to Texas with my mom, he said he knew what had happened because he was in the car with Tom when Tom told me he went to see Bob. Rinder told me he liked Bob. He didn't say much else because we were distracted at a coffee shop and it wasn't easy to talk. Also, he had a friend with him and maybe Rinder didn't want to say too much in front of that guy.

The next morning, Jim's sister called me and said that Bob had emailed her and told her to quit talking to Jim's ex, Lori. "She is crazy and sent someone here to my house." He added, "If you continue to talk to Lori then I can't talk to you anymore."

Jim's sister was really surprised how Bob knew we were talking. Then Jim called his sister and said the same thing; that I was crazy and to stay away from me or he would have to disconnect from her. Then Bob and Jim called their sister-in-law, who was also talking to me and trying to help reunite me and my kids. They gave her the same speech. Both of the ladies told me they couldn't talk to me anymore or they would lose their brothers. It was just another example of the pervasive hatred of Scientology's cruel Disconnection Policy.

So I no longer had the support from the sisters. They felt bad that they couldn't talk to me anymore and they both told me not to give up.

On October 11, 2011, Mark Bunker released a segment of our interview. That same day, Tony Ortega (chief editor of *The Village Voice*) wrote an article and shared my interview segment. At that time, Tony was waiting for me to share my full story with him. I think the media exposure helped other people know the truth about Scientology's abuses, but speaking out made me an even bigger target. I felt safer knowing Tony was always there, going after Scientology and its ongoing crimes against humanity. I think the security of knowing I had a reporter to share this craziness the church was doing, someone who would make it public quickly, helped me stay strong.

I soon found out something terrible about Jeremy, and it was horrible how I had to learn what happened.

Chapter Fifteen

A Motorbike Accident on Facebook

It was October 18, 2011, a Tuesday evening. I was having dinner with my husband at one of our favorite places in San Jose near our house. During dinner, I glanced down at my cell phone and saw a Facebook notification that my cousin posted. It said, "Moto Friends....please be careful! 2 Major bad accidents in 1 week is too much for me and this time hitting too close to home. Please say a prayer for my cousin in the ER right now! :("

When I saw this, my heart sank and I felt sick to my stomach. I had a bad feeling it was my son. Then my cousin later posted: *"Jeremy took the triple as he always does, but landed short, Turner said he flew, bike hit him twice. He tried to jump off bike but his feet got hooked on the bars. :(... Alan and Turner both said it was a really brutal site. [sic] Prayer's he is ok!"*

At that moment I knew it was my son who was injured and I was terrified! I called my cousin and left a message for her to call me ASAP. My husband and I immediately left the restaurant and I went home with my mind racing about what to do. I was thinking how I could find out if he was okay and what ER he was in. I was not called when my son was being rushed to the hospital with serious injuries. What an awful way to find out your son is in the ER, by a Facebook post! Thank God my cousin posted it or I wouldn't have known for a while. All I could think about was what ER he was in.

I remembered that when Jeremy had a previous serious motorcycle accident he was flown to Santa Clara Valley Medical Hospital so I called there first. I asked the ER if my son Jeremy Leake had been admitted and they confirmed he had been, but I could get no more information. I called my father and stepmom and asked them if they could meet me at the ER. The hospital was about fifteen minutes away.

When my parents and I arrived, I went up to the ER window first and told them I was Jeremy Leake's mom and my son just got admitted and I asked if he was okay. The person at the desk said they could not give me any information on my son. I was shocked that they couldn't even let me know if my son was okay! For Christ's sake, I was his mom! I begged them to let me see him. I'm sure my call to the ER alerted Jim Leake and Jessica that I was on my way. Despite the fact that Jeremy's life might be in the balance, Jim, Jessica and Jeremy were abiding by the rules of Scientology's Disconnection Policy, which was to cut off all ties with me because I had left Scientology, and if they didn't they would be faced with the probability of getting kicked out of their organization. I never thought Scientology Disconnection could keep apart a mom and son when her son is in the ER, but because Jeremy was eighteen and no longer a minor, I was not able to see him. I was completely devastated, not knowing if he was even okay, let alone not being able to see him. It was a mother's worst nightmare!

My parents and I were in the ER waiting room, trying to get a grasp on this situation and what to do. I noticed I had a voicemail message from my cousin that sounded extremely upset, "Lori, please don't go to the hospital. They are freaking out on me right now. I told them I did not contact you, but they are freaking out. They said they know that you're on the way, I guess? I don't know why you're not answering right now."

My cousin then texted me that my daughter Jessica had texted her that Jim was . . . "furious" that she had made the Facebook post that enabled me to find out that my son had sustained life-threatening injuries. I went up to the ER desk again and asked to speak to a nurse. I asked her if she could please ask my son if I could see him. I was told, "Your son does not want to see you."

"Can you at least give me his status?"

The nurse replied, "No, your son is eighteen, and by the privacy laws we're not allowed to give out any information."

I told my parents I had to try to find a way to see if Jeremy was okay. I decided to go around to the back of the ER and I saw a different nurse coming out. I told him that my son Jeremy was in the ER and quickly explained Scientology's policy of disconnection and that I just wanted to know how bad my son got hurt and if he was okay. By the time I finished explaining, I was crying. The nurse could clearly see I was a mom who was very worried about her son. He told me he couldn't give me any information, but said to write a note and he would give it to Jeremy for me.

I found a pen and some paper and quickly wrote a note to my son. "Jeremy, this is your mom. I'm here. I want to see you, and love you very much. Are you okay?"

The nurse took the note to Jeremy, then came back and told me that Jeremy said to tell me he was all right, but that he couldn't see anyone. The nurse also said that Jeremy was alone in his room because his father and sister were talking to the doctor. Phew, good timing or I probably would not have heard back from Jeremy.

I was relieved, because I knew that my son was okay. I told my parents to go home and get some sleep and that I would let them know anything as soon as I got any information. After a night of a minimal amount of sleep, I called my friend who was still in Scientology. I told her what had happened and that I couldn't see my son in the ER. I told her I'd been keeping Tony Ortega, a reporter on Scientology, updated on my disconnection and that I was going to disclose to him this horrific situation that I could not see my son, proof of the cruel disconnection policy Scientology enforced. I related how Scientology was keeping me away from my son in the hospital after he had a serious accident. She said she would call Kathy True (a Scientology spokesperson) and tell her what was going on and that this was going to be really bad PR for the church if they didn't let me see my son. She was going to tell Kathy she'd better let me see my son in the hospital today or if not it would be a huge "PR flap." Scientology would generally do anything to prevent looking bad in the press.

I was learning to use the media, which was basically the only weapon I had in fighting for my kids. One of the first times I found out about Tony Ortega and his blog posts was when I was at Marty's in April 2011 when the Squirrel Busters harassed us and Marty wrote about it and shared the Squirrel Busters video. That day, Ortega wrote a blog post and named me and Marty. Then I started following his posts in *The Village Voice*. Shortly after that, I sent him a friend request on Facebook.

In the summer of 2011, I talked to Tony on the phone and told him that I was writing my short disconnection story and asked if he was interested in sharing it. He said yes, he was. Then I did the Mark Bunker interview in the fall of 2011 and Tony asked me if he could share my interview. He asked me if I was done with my story, but I wasn't done with it at that time.

I was still beyond upset so before I went back to the hospital, I posted about not being able to see my son on Facebook. Tony private-messaged me and said he was so sorry and asked if he could call me. We talked and I shared everything that had happened and said he could post an article about the situation. From then on, we remained in touch.

I really liked Tony as a reporter and chose to keep him updated on everything I did to try to reconnect with my kids. Tony wrote around a dozen posts about my situation and became a huge support. I was grateful for his support that I could share heartbreaking situations with him. I called him when I was really upset about my kids and he helped me so much by listening. I also ran some of my ideas by him as I was trying to reconnect with my kids. I always chose Tony first to share any new developments, or any fair-game attacks.

So back to Jeremy and the accident. I picked up my mom and we headed to the hospital. I was determined to see my son; nothing was going to stand in my way. Maybe he would want to see me. I thought I'd ask the nurse again.

Once I got to the hospital, I was able to find out that Jeremy was scheduled for surgery that morning. I got to the hospital before Jim and Jessica arrived, so I was able to get lots of information about Jeremy. I'm not sure if my friend had called Kathy True or not. I found out Jeremy had fractured his femur and collarbone. They told me his surgery was scheduled in a few hours. While I was waiting, I saw Jim and Jessica arrive and head directly to the nurses' station. They hadn't noticed Mom and me yet.

Then Jim walked over to me and said, "You can go. Jeremy is going to be fine."

I said, "Absolutely not, I'm staying!"

He walked away with an irritated expression. I told the nurse that I would like to talk to the doctor before the surgery if I could. The doctor called me, my ex, and my daughter over and as I walked by, Jessica said, "Hi, Mom."

That was the first time I had seen my daughter in eight months. I listened to what the doctor said about my son's injuries and the surgeries planned. Jeremy was in the pre–surgery area.

My father showed up and I updated him on his grandson's condition. I shared with my dad that today was better, because so far no one was stopping me from getting information on Jeremy and that I had spoken with the doctor and that my ex and Jessica were there.

After three hours of anxiously waiting in the recovery room for my son to get out of surgery, we learned his operation went well. He had a nail in his femur with pins on each side holding the bones together. His collarbone was broken. The doctor said it should heal naturally. While I was waiting to see him, my mom and I walked around the hospital and luckily saw Jeremy go by on a gurney with Jim and Jessica by his side. They did not see us. Mom and I followed Jeremy to his room without them noticing. We waited outside by the elevator for a few minutes and then went in to see Jeremy. Jim was near his bedside and Jessica was at the end of his bed. As Jim saw me walk in, he asked our son if he wanted to see me.

Before Jeremy could finish answering, I went over to my son and said, "Hi, Jeremy. I've been here for you all day and I'm so glad you're doing well. I'm going to leave now so there is not a problem for you. I hope you get well real fast and I love you so very much."

Jeremy looked at me and said, "I love you."

Jessica was talking to the nurse. I went up to her and hugged her and said, "I miss you and love you." Jessica hugged me back then my mom gave Jessica a hug.

We decided to leave the hospital since I knew my staying there would stress my son because he was being controlled and forced to follow Scientology's cruel policy. I wanted him to heal without being affected by the stress of disconnection. He was in enough pain as it was.

During the day, while I was waiting to see my son, I told Tony Ortega he could share what happened on *The Village Voice*, the blog on which he was the chief editor. The title of the article was "Scientology's 'Disconnection': Lori Hodgson, Ex-Church Member, Kept from Scientologist Son After Serious Wreck (UPDATED)"

Tony kept everyone following my story updated throughout the day. I was doing everything possible to get Scientology to let me see my son. I strongly feel Tony's reporting helped me see him because if Scientology didn't then it would have been an even bigger PR flap and I'm sure they didn't want that.

I called early every morning so I could speak to Jeremy's nurse before his dad arrived. I was able to get updates that way and was at ease because Jeremy was recovering well. He was released to go home after a few days. Jim took him home; Jeremy was living with him. I did not have my son's cell number and none of the family did, either. I asked my stepmom to call Jim to see how Jeremy was and ask if she could talk to him. Jim answered and he passed the phone to our son. Jeremy seemed happy to hear from his grandma and he told her he was healing well. She said she loved him and missed him.

That was it, the only information I got on my son.

In November 2011, my best friend Beth made me two yellow ribbons, one for Jessica and one for Jeremy, to tie on my two front yard trees. The ribbons were a symbol for my children to come home. I shared the pic on my Facebook page along with the song "Tie a Yellow Ribbon 'round the Old Oak

Tree," by Tony Orlando. I planned to keep the ribbons on my trees till my children returned.

I also heard from my cousin that around this time Jessica and Justin broke up and Jessica got rid of her apartment and moved to Morgan Hill to live with her dad and her brother.

I would always share my messages to my children on my Facebook page just in case Jessica or Jeremy could see them somehow through a friend's account, because Scientology made them block me and my family.

Later on in November, I got a call from Lisa Bartley, a producer for ABC7 in Los Angeles, California. She found out about me via Tony Ortega's writing and wanted to do my disconnection story. She was very compassionate and supportive and wanted to share my story. This would be my second TV interview. She sent two cameramen to my house and we filmed in my son Jeremy's room via Skype with Lisa.

We started the interview and when she asked me about Jeremy's recent motorcycle accident and how I was kept from seeing him due to Scientology's disconnection policy, I lost it. I cried for several minutes. I could barely finish the interview. I was still shook up from this recent time with my son and how I was prevented from being there with him like it was natural for a mother to do. The interview did not go well as I was too emotional, and it never got aired. Before my interview that day, my Facebook page got hacked and a few of my close friends' Facebooks were hacked, too. I do not feel this was a coincidence.

I settled into the dark reality that this would be an ongoing battle. The so-called "church" of Scientology would do anything to keep my sweet children from me.

Chapter Sixteen

My First Christmas without My Kids

It was the middle of December 2011, and I was out Christmas shopping at the mall where I used to take my kids. Every store reminded me of my son and daughter and I would just hold back the tears. Not being able to be with my kids this Christmas was heartrending. We loved the holiday season and would always Christmas shop together. I decided to get my kids Christmas presents at a store called PacSun. I could barely stay focused on picking out their presents; my tears were making it difficult to see. I came home and wrapped their presents in Christmas bags with a loving Christmas card inside each one.

Now I was contemplating how to get the presents to my kids. They both lived with their father at this time in Morgan Hill, about thirty minutes from me. I knew I couldn't go see them when Jim was home, as the FBI told me to stay away from him, so I tried my best to do that. I called my friend Beth and asked her if she would go with me to Morgan Hill in the early evening. I had just found out that Jim was out of town in Austin, Texas, doing some work, so this was my opportunity to see my kids. I discussed my plan with two people, my good friends Paul and Beth. After talking to them, I decided it would be best to go with Beth. She and I planned what we were going to do over the phone then met a few days later.

Earlier that day, my friend Paul said there was a Scientologist outside his house spying on him. He called me and told me what was going on.

I said, "Maybe Scientology thinks I'm taking you to see my kids." This was another time I felt my phone was being tapped, most likely by Scientology operatives.

I picked Beth up at her apartment around four-thirty. We got to Morgan Hill around five p.m. We didn't notice anyone following us. I was hoping the timing would be perfect, when the kids would be getting home from work. We got to their trailer about five-thirty and I had the Christmas presents in my hands. I knocked on the door several times. No answer. We waited about thirty minutes. Finally, I wrote my kids a loving message of Merry Christmas and left the presents on the front porch.

As we left, down the long street we saw a car approaching. We thought it might be a Scientologist following us. As the vehicle approached, we noticed it was my son in his tan truck. I went real slow so he could see me. He was really surprised and immediately got on his phone. He went to the end of the street and turned around. I turned around to go meet him. As we were approaching each other, I drove slowly, giving him a chance to slow down and talk to me. He went by me while he was on the phone and kept going, drove to the end of the street and headed off into the hills.

I wasn't going to chase him. I clearly wanted him to see that I was just trying to talk to him and give him a chance to see me if he wanted. I couldn't believe he didn't stop. I feel he was on the phone either with his father or a Scientology operative who was manipulating his every action. This was so sad that my son couldn't stop for a moment to talk to his mom.

I was tearful the whole way home. I'm glad I had left the presents with a note so they would both see I was still their mom and doing everything I could to show them I was here and that I loved them very much. I got no acknowledgement from either of my kids for the presents and I didn't expect one. Christmas came and I could barely be with my family. I wept privately in the bathroom so my family didn't see the pain I was in. All I could think about was my kids and how I ached for their presence. It was a grief-stricken Christmas.

I thought about all my Christmases in the past. I was baptized Lutheran and celebrated all the holidays with my family. After I became a Scientologist, my family still celebrated Christmas, Easter, and the rest of the holidays. My mom and I believed in God even when we were Scientologists. My dad's side was Catholic so I celebrated all the holidays with them, too. After I married Jim, I noticed he wasn't that into celebrating the holidays or birthdays like I was, but he would still participate. When we had kids, I continued the special holiday get-togethers with all sides of my family. My kids were raised celebrating Christmas, Easter, and we always made a big event out of everyone's birthday. The family on all sides would celebrate.

After Jim and I got divorced, he said that I could have the kids on all the holidays and for their birthdays because they were used to the parties and

Jim was not that into making a big thing about any of those days. So all Christmases, Thanksgivings, and Easters meant fun times and celebrations. Both my kids loved holidays and birthdays and spending quality family time together. I spoiled my kids like crazy with presents, even when I was broke while living with Jim. I somehow managed to make it awesome for my kids. For that reason, I was sure they both would really miss their family on holidays and birthdays, but it was obvious that Scientology was doing its best to quash any joy they'd ever felt for such occasions with us.

A couple of weeks after Christmas, CR's father took us to Hawaii. I was excited about the trip, but my heart was missing Jessica and Jeremy. We got to Kauai and stayed in a lovely oceanfront condo. We went zip-lining, my first time doing this, and I loved it. Then I began thinking about how much my kids would love zip-lining and how much I missed them. We stayed about ten days. During that time, my daughter had texted my husband that she had returned our Christmas presents and left them on our porch. CR did not tell me this until we got back home as he didn't want to ruin my trip. I was texting both my kids pictures I took in Hawaii and telling them I wished they were with me on vacation and how much I loved them and missed them. My texts were showing as delivered, but I got no responses.

While we were in Hawaii, my neighbor saw the presents on the porch and hid them in the bushes. My mom went over to my house to get the mail and my neighbor saw her and told her about the presents in the bushes. Mom took the returned presents to her house and was not going to tell me they had returned them. She just knew it would break my heart. My neighbor and mom decided it would be best not to tell me. That evening when I finished unpacking from our trip, CR showed me Jessica's text. I read it and was crushed. I knew that Scientology and their father must have ordered them to return the presents. I know my kids would never be that cruel. Scientology probably knew about my trip and planned this cruel scheme to ruin it. I'm so glad my mom and husband did not tell me when I was in Hawaii. I called her and told her that CR had shown me Jessica's text. Mom told me she had the presents so I asked her if she would give them to me. I put them in Jeremy's closet for a time when my kids came home.

I had left Jeremy's room the way it was from the day he was forced to disconnect from me. He loved his room. I always let my kids decorate their own rooms. After Jim and I divorced, I hired a painter and we all got to choose the color of our rooms. Jeremy chose red. He had two red walls and two white walls. Jessica chose blue and had two blue walls and two white walls. I chose yellow. The three of us chose yellow for the outside of our house, with a red front door.

I couldn't change Jeremy's room. I left up his dirt bike posters; his San Jose Sharks stick autographed by Mike Ricci, a professional San Jose Sharks hockey player; his trophies; a cool surfboard we got him; and all the clothes hanging in his closet. I also kept the same bedspread that he picked out when I got him a new bed when he came home from the Sea Org. Since Jessica had moved out and had her own apartment, we used her room as an office.

As much as I tried to preserve the past, however, it couldn't erase the pain of the present. I just tried to keep busy and figure anything I could do to get my kids back. That was about to get harder.

Chapter Seventeen

My Kids Move to Texas

In February 2012, I found out that my ex was moving my kids far away to Austin, Texas. I couldn't believe it; Jessica and Jeremy were the epitome of California kids. I heard that Jim told my daughter he would get her her own preschool. I have no idea what he told Jeremy. I wrote my son a letter that he did not have to move, saying he could stay with me and I would help him with college or a vocational school if he liked. I never heard back from either of my kids. No goodbyes, nothing! They moved to Austin in April 2012. I was heartsick and knew how hard this was going to be to try to reunite with my kids with us being thousands of miles apart. I had no address for them, no phone numbers, no emails.

In May, I heard from a mutual friend of my kids that Jessica was working at a preschool and Jeremy was working at a restaurant. I was happy that they were not working for Scientology again. I also heard that summer through the media that Katie Holmes had decided to leave Tom Cruise. I decided to share my disconnection story with Katie's father. I found out his name and learned that he was an attorney so I searched on the Internet for his law firm. I located his email and sent him my story. I'm not sure if he received it, but I hope he did.

In June, my son turned nineteen. I couldn't even send him a birthday present because I had no address. I posted a loving message on my Facebook wall, wishing him a happy birthday and saying how much I loved and missed him.

I decided to get my first tattoo on my son's birthday. I had always wanted to get a tattoo and there was no better day to do that. I got the Batman symbol on my lower back. I had been a Batman fan since I was a kid so it was perfect.

Plus, I was fighting this cruel organization that had taken my kids from me so a crime fighter like Batman really fit. From that day on, my mom nicknamed me Batman and called herself Robin. We were quite the dynamic duo. Getting a tattoo is not an easy process; it hurts like crazy, then there is about two weeks of after-care, but to me it was worth it because I got it on my son's birthday.

On my mom's July 4th birthday, we were terribly sad about my kids being gone and disconnected from us. They were all we could think about. We shared pictures on our Facebook pages hoping that somehow the kids could see our posts, and maybe that would remind them of all the fun July 4ths we'd had together.

The following day, I went dirt bike riding with CR. We loved to ride dirt bikes. I had a KTM 250 and my husband had a Kawasaki 450. We went riding at Cow Mountain, which was only fifteen minutes from our lake house. Cow Mountain is where my son and I did our first fifty-five mile Enduro race together before the disconnection. Jeremy was around fifteen years old then. He did great, placing seventh in his class, while I couldn't even finish. I only made it thirty miles and the sweepers—the guys that help the ones having trouble—sent me back. I was proud of my son, though.

CR and I started riding that day and as soon as we got on the fire road I started crying so hard I could barely see beyond my tears. We pulled over and my husband saw what an emotional mess I was. He told me to take off my helmet and come and sit down near the side of the road. He was always very good at getting me out of my depression. He knew how to change the subject and that's what he did. He started discussing erosion control. He specializes in this subject with his work. After five minutes, I told him I was fine and ready to ride. I told him if he ever saw me crying again while dirt-biking to start giving me a lecture on erosion control and that would get me back on my bike before he could count to ten.

In August 2012, my friend Beth and her two boys came up to the lake. I had bought a Batman costume and told my husband, Beth, and the boys that I would try water-skiing in it. I put it on over my life jacket, which was perfect because then I looked like a weightlifter guy. I got up, but the eye holes had moved over. I couldn't see, but was still able to ski. I guess when you've been water-skiing since the age of four, you can ski blindfolded.

Beth's son Danny used our Go Pro Camera and made a YouTube video of me skiing in my Batman costume with the tune "Eye of the Tiger" in the background. I shared it on my Facebook wall hoping that my kids would see it and get a chuckle out of that. No matter what I was doing, I was always thinking about my kids.

On November 3, 2012, I decided to write my kids an open letter since I had no way of reaching them directly. I thought maybe they would see it through people sharing. I posted it on my Facebook wall and Tony Ortega shared it for me on *The Village Voice* blog. By this time, my kids had been in Austin for eight months and I missed them terribly.

Dear Jessica and Jeremy,

I have no way of reaching you directly, so I'm giving this a try. I'm asking all of my friends, family, and anyone else that gets this letter to please pass it on to each of you.

Despite what you might have been told, I am doing well in all areas of my life. The only thing missing is the two of you. I am still the same mom who loves you both very much.

But I want you to understand that I will never go back into the Church of Scientology. You have both asked me to talk to the International Justice Chief and get back in good standing with the church. I cannot agree to this. I am not a part of the church anymore and do not have to go by their rules. I am free now to think for myself and do what I think is best.

I don't agree with the church's Disconnection Policy that you both are following, forcing you to stay away from me. Your grandmother and I will not disconnect from you, and we will continue to love you.

I really want you both to think long and hard about this disconnection that is keeping you away from us. Do you both really never want to see me and your grandmother again? Do you never want to see the rest of the family because your grandmother and I won't go back into the church?

If you both want to stay in Scientology we respect that, but at the same time you need to respect that we don't want to be a part of it anymore. If I were in your shoes I would never agree to this disconnection. I would tell the church that I would remain a part of my family's life. I would never allow the church to force me to disconnect from the people I love.

Your grandfather is 75, your grandmother is turning 75, and I am turning 50. Time is going by fast and we should all enjoy many more good times together.

You both know the reasons why I resigned from the church. It was mainly because of the way you were heavily recruited to be on staff or in the Sea Org at only 15 years old. I wanted you both to stay in school and get a full education. I fought with the church because my parental rights were being violated. I also saw what you both went through while being recruited and what you both went through while being in the Sea Org. I wrote everything that happened in "A Mother's Heartbreak," which it would be good if you both read so you can really see what happened.

Forever loving you both,
Your Mom

Thanksgiving and Christmas 2012 I was still without my kids. I got through these holidays, but it was tough. I'm sure it was rough for my kids, too. Ever since the disconnection, the holidays were not the same without my sweet children. We celebrated the holidays as best we could and decorated for them, too. My daughter loved Thanksgiving and always asked her Nonie to make deviled eggs. It was our family tradition to go to Christmas in Saratoga the Friday after Thanksgiving. We enjoyed looking in all the stores and having hot pumpkin streusel. Without my children, I stopped decorating for the holidays. It was just too sad of a time for me without my children.

On February 27, 2013, I wrote an open letter to a Los Angeles crisis management specialist, Michael Sitrick. Sitrick was hired by Scientology to help with its public relations image. I wanted him to know the truth about Scientology and how they ripped apart my family. I was hoping the letter would move him emotionally so he could help me get my family back together. Here is my open letter that I sent to him:

Dear Mr. Sitrick,

My name is Lori Hodgson. I am a former Scientologist and a mother who is going through a heartbreaking disconnection with my two children, Jessica and Jeremy Leake. I am writing to you in hopes that you can help bring my children back home to me. I have heard that your company "Sitrick and Company" may be assisting the Church of Scientology. If it is true and you are working with Scientology, I would like to share my disconnection story with you.

The Church of Scientology states that they do not have a Disconnection Policy. I am living proof that this is a lie. I am currently going through the biggest heartbreak of my life. I love my Jeremy, age 19, and my Jessica, age 22, immensely and I cannot even talk to them. The Church of Scientology has turned my own children completely against me and has broken our family apart.

I resigned from the Church of Scientology in August 2010. My main reason for leaving Scientology was because of what happened with my two children when they both turned 15. They were recruited, at 15 years old, behind my back, to work for Scientology. I was strongly opposed to this as I wanted my children to finish high school and get a proper education. I fought this with Scientology and my parental rights were very much violated. I got broken down by the COS's recruiters and I was coerced into letting them join.

In fact, with Jeremy's recruiting cycle, I was on pain pills recovering from a knee replacement surgery during my son's recruitment for the Sea Org. The Sea Org promised me that Jeremy would have his schooling, get his driver's license, and be able to come home to visit and talk to me whenever we wanted. All these promises were broken! They were lies! Then, when Jeremy wanted to leave the Sea Org, the COS made him sign a 3- Million-Dollar Gag Contract to never discuss what happened when he was in the SO. Jeremy was only 16 years old when he had to sign this. He never even got a copy. What does Jeremy know that is worth a 3–million-dollar threat? If this was your son wouldn't you be concerned? I did go public with the COS's abuses committed on my children and myself.

The COS has manipulated my children to disconnect from me and their grandparents. We can't talk to them. We don't even know their address or have a contact phone number. Jeremy was not allowed to call me or his grandpa and he was made to change his cell number. My father is heartbroken about his disconnected grandchildren.

Please, Mr. Sitrick, can you help me get my children back? Scientology is not telling the truth about disconnection. They have their Disconnection Policy in full force. I am going through this cruel disconnection currently. Below are some links to my Disconnection nightmare. I hope you have the opportunity to read them. If you have any questions, my cell is .... and my email is ....

Sincerely,
Lori Hodgson

Unfortunately, I never heard back from Michael Sitrick. At least I'd shown that I would continue to try and fight for my kids and that I was not afraid to communicate to anyone. I was a Mama Bear who would try to get through all obstacles for my kids. Which led me to my next move, traveling to Texas to find them.

Chapter Eighteen

Gone to Texas

By May 2013, I hadn't seen my daughter or son since October 2011 when Jeremy was in the hospital from his bad motorcycle accident. I tried many times to try to connect to my kids by email, phone, and sending messages via my friends and family. I never got a response. When I was able to get one of my children's phone numbers and tried calling, they had to change their numbers. I had no address of where either one of my kids was living. I had heard they lived with their father.

I did find out that my son got a job at a restaurant in Austin, Texas, and I asked my stepmom, Jeremy's grandma, to call him. At this time, both kids talked to their grandparents, but not to my mom. My stepmom called and Jeremy came to the phone, but said he couldn't talk because he was working. She asked if he could please call her back. It took about two weeks until she got a return call, but Jeremy had his sister call. My stepmom and dad were very happy to hear from the kids and asked if they could come visit. Jessica said they couldn't because they had plans.

Shortly thereafter, I found out Jeremy quit his job at the restaurant and got a job at a motorcycle store in Austin. I asked my uncle to go check on Jeremy, as he lived in Austin, too. My uncle said Jeremy was looking good, but seemed nervous that he had visited him. Then I had a friend drop off a nice loving card for Jeremy stating that I loved him and missed him. Jeremy took the card, but asked my friend to leave.

I couldn't stand being away from my children for so long so I asked my mom if she would go with me to Austin to try to see the kids. She said yes and we started to plan our trip. We had to be very careful how we went about our travel arrangements since Scientology was keeping an eye on me. I was pretty sure Scientology had broken into my social media and had gotten my itinerary in the past since the Squirrel Busters had followed me to Corpus Christi. I was very cautious by now. I talked with a friend about how to go about getting my itinerary and lodging arrangements set up so Scientology could not track me. I also turned off my GPS to my mom's and my own cells and I got a throwaway phone to stay in touch with my family in California.

The day before I left my lake home, I took some pictures of myself at the lake with my dogs. I posted those pics the day I caught my flight to Austin to throw Scientology off and have them think I was still at the lake. I was doing everything possible to prevent Scientology from intervening in my reunion with my kids.

I had my son's work address and knew we had to get right over to his work as soon as we got our rental car in a way that we could not be tracked. We then used the GPS in the rental car to get to the Austin police station. Since I was working with the authorities, I had been advised to let them know if I was traveling and especially if I tried to go to Texas to reach my children. My mom and I checked in with the Austin police and I told them I was here to see my son and to show him that I'm fine, since I heard that Scientology had told my children I was crazy and doing awful. I wanted to let my son know I love him and wanted to put our family back together. After checking in with the police, we headed directly to my son's work, about a twenty-minute drive.

We drove by first to see if I could spot his truck and we did. I was extremely nervous to see my son and I kept on driving. I was afraid of him rejecting me after I came all this way. Mom encouraged me to turn around. We pulled into the parking lot of Woods Fun Center. There were large glass windows and I was worried Jeremy would see us before I could talk to him and he might leave or not come out to see me. I sat there in my car and told my mom I was scared to death. My heart was pounding and I was sweating. She told me to take some big breaths, which I did then she said, "We're going in!"

We got out of our rental and walked in. I knew from a friend that Jeremy worked at the parts counter and that it was in the back far left of the store. My mom and I approached the counter and I didn't see Jeremy. I saw two employees and asked one of them, "Is Jeremy here?" As I asked, I saw my son eating his lunch in a side room. We both looked at each other and he almost choked on his food. He looked completely surprised to see me. This was the first time I had laid eyes on my son in over a year.

Jeremy seemed happy to see me. He came right over and gave me a big hug. "What are you doing here?" he asked.

"We came here to see you."

Jeremy looked incredulous. "You came here to see me?"

"Yeah, I took off six days so Nonie and I could come and see you."

Jeremy looked at his grandmother and just said, "Wow!"

Mom and I asked Jeremy how he was doing and he said he was doing well. I told him, "I miss you and I love you."

He replied, "I miss you too, Mom. I love you."

To lighten up our uncomfortableness, I told him we had brought a shopping list. I knew he was working at a motorcycle shop and thought he could help me pick out some motorcycle things. He laughed!

We continued to talk. I didn't want to bring up Scientology so I talked about other things. I told him that Nonie moved to Clear Lake and bought a home on the lake and that my husband, CR, and I had bought the place across the street from Papa's. He was excited to hear that. I told Jeremy that we would love him to visit. And I told him that Papa and Grandma Leanie, Jeremy's other grandparents, were taking us all to Hawaii and that we would love him and his sister to come with us.

My mom decided to give us some time alone so she excused herself and went to the restroom. I knew this was the time to be more direct and try to reconcile our relationship.

I said, "Jeremy, I just want to be your mom, I just want to be your friend."

Jeremy replied, "You know what to do to fix that!" He was referring to the "A to E steps," which, as I explained earlier, are what Scientology requires ex-members to do to be able to get their disconnected family and friends back.

I said, "Jeremy, I can't go back in the church. To do that I would have to do the 'A to E steps' and I would have to say I lied. I didn't lie and I can't do that."

"Mom, I don't want to talk about that here."

"I would have to do their counseling and I don't want to do that," I told him. "I don't care if you don't want to move back to California. I just want to be your mom and visit and be friends."

Jeremy just repeated, "You know what to do to fix it."

"I can't do those steps! There just has to be another way. Let's get your dad and we can all talk about this to find another way that we all agree on."

Jeremy seemed surprised. "You would meet with my dad?"

"Yes, I will meet with your dad." Then I gave him the number of the throwaway phone I got for my trip. "There has to be another way besides my going back in the church for us to be together. Don't you think there's another way so we can be back together?"

He was hesitant then responded with, "Maybe."

After discussing our new plan about meeting with his dad, Jeremy seemed happier. He and I finished my shopping and he rang me up for my purchases. I had Jeremy help me select a green motorcycle jersey since CR loved Kawasaki and their green colors, and then helped me pick out a motorcycle tank top and some socks.

My son and I both had a passion for dirt bikes. We used to ride often together and had a blast. We continued talking about my new tattoos, which he said he liked. I also mentioned that his dog Rocky was doing well and that we got a new little dog, a pug named Otto. I showed him pictures. Jeremy could clearly see that I was not crazy like his dad and other Scientologists said I was and that I was doing well, except that I missed him and his sister Jessica very much. He never tried to text his dad while I was there, which seemed like a miracle. I was so happy that it had gone so much better than I thought it would and I got to spend forty-five quality minutes with my son.

I told Jeremy that Nonie and I were staying in Austin for the next six days and asked him to join us for dinner that night, and I would love for him to bring his new girlfriend whom I hadn't met yet, and Jessica and her boyfriend. I asked him to please call me and let me know if he could meet that night. I also left him with a present. I had a special motorcycle keychain made for him and told him I had a matching one. He liked it.

As I left, he gave me one more hug and we said we loved each other again.

My mom was thrilled because she got three hugs from her grandson and with one of the hugs he grabbed her and hugged her tight.

I was sad we had to leave, but I knew I didn't want to overwhelm him by staying too long and getting him in trouble with his job.

When Mom and I got in the car and drove off towards our hotel, she said, "I really saw the love between you and Jeremy and that he seems really sad and misses his family." She was also happy that Jeremy saw that I wasn't crazy and that I was in great shape and doing well. "He knows you love him and wants to work this out," she added.

We both felt very positive about the visit, but both had a feeling we might not see him again on this trip. We tried to stay positive.

We checked in at our hotel and all I could think about was how great it was to hug my son and talk to him. I kept going over it again and again in my head. It was getting past dinnertime and no call from Jeremy. I bet his dad or Scientology operatives found out and insisted that he not call or meet with us.

I was upset at not hearing from my son so I called Tony Ortega and told him about our visit. Then my mom and I were both exhausted, so we turned in early.

The next couple of days we met with some Facebook friends who were also former Scientologists. We noticed a few people watching us and following us around town. On one of the days we met my friends Marty and Mosey Rathbun in San Antonio. On our way, we were being followed by a black SUV. We ditched them, but noticed when we got to the restaurant where we were meeting our friends there were a man and a woman on top of a bridge near where we were sitting, taking pictures of us.

Marty and Mosey called and said they were running late because they were also being followed. When they arrived, we had a fun visit but the Rathbuns informed us that there was a man sitting behind us who was watching us. Despite all this, it was great seeing our friends. The visit reminded me of when we were being watched by the Squirrel Busters, but much less threatening.

The following day was Mother's Day and I was hoping to hear from my kids. I had my good friend send Jeremy a message asking him and Jessica to join us for a Mother's Day dinner at Guero's, a Mexican restaurant in Austin. I wasn't holding my breath that they would come, but I strongly believed they would.

Mom and I took the shuttle there and got a seat by the entrance. We waited and waited and they never came. I was crushed as I had let my expectations and hopes get the best of me. I wept quietly throughout our dinner. Mom and I had a very sad Mother's Day dinner. Always there for me, she stayed supportive and kept me going with hope and encouraged me to never give up. I loved my mom with all my heart and was very grateful to have her by my side. I couldn't have done this without her.

We said our goodbyes to Austin and were grateful we at least got to see Jeremy. I wish I could have seen my daughter, too, but I had no phone number or address for Jessica. I only knew where my son worked. It was a sad flight back home. I continued to go over my visit in my mind and wondered over and over if there was anything else I could have done to reunite with my children, such as stay longer, go back to his workplace, something else. Nothing helped. I was broken-hearted again.

Chapter Nineteen

Meeting Fellow-Fighters

The summer of 2013 was another sad season without my kids. Memorial Day was always the kickoff of summer for my family and fun times at the lake. Jeremy and Jessica loved Memorial Day weekend vacations with us. We all stayed at my Dad and my stepmom Leanie's house. My kids called their other grandma Leanie. We boated, went water-skiing, and Jeremy and Jessica wake-boarded, went to the movies, and put together puzzles and played cards. Leanie and my dad would cook the yummiest dinners, too.

This Memorial Day was another time at the lake without my kids and I had a terrible sadness missing them and thinking of all the fun memories we had together. No matter what I did, my mind was on my kids. We took a boat ride and I would just stare off at the lake and the beautiful mountains surrounding the lake, visualizing having my kids back with us. Many times, I would hold back my tears so my family didn't get sad all over again.

In June, my son turned twenty and I sent a birthday present to his work. I called the shop to see if he had received my present and they told me that he knew about it, but he hadn't taken it yet. It was sitting in the back office. When I heard that, my heart dropped. There was nothing worse than continually being torn apart from my son. Jeremy was not allowed to have any connection with me, even accepting gifts, unless I went back and did the Scientology steps. At least he knew I cared and thought about him on his birthday.

July 4th came and we celebrated Mom's birthday. We thought of the kids and reminisced about all our wonderful memories on 4th of July vacations. Somehow, we managed to have a wonderful day celebrating, but missed the kids a lot. I was hoping that maybe they would call their Nonie and wish her a happy birthday, but that didn't happen. I always tried to think positive and believe that the cruel disconnection would end soon.

Later in July, I decided to make a card the size of a business card that I could hand out to people. The card would have my name and contact info and explain my cause to reunite with my children and how I was fighting the Church of Scientology's despicable policy of disconnection. I made two hundred and fifty cards and handed out many. Any chance I got, I shared how Scientology ripped apart my family and explained my fight to get my children back. People were very receptive.

The same month, I got a call from my dear friend Karen de la Carriere. She asked me if I was interested in sharing my story by doing videos at her Los Angeles studio. She posted the interviews on her YouTube site "Surviving Scientology." I decided to take her up on this great opportunity and asked my best friend Beth to go with me to Los Angeles. We set up a time for the end of July. I kept it very quiet as I did not want to be harassed again by Scientology.

We met with Karen and her husband Jeffrey for dinner the evening before. I shared my story with both of them. The next morning, I got up early and Beth and I went to one of my favorite places, Starbucks, to go over my timeline of events and to write down some notes. We found a nice Starbucks on Hollywood Boulevard. Beth was a huge support to me and helped me get my notes organized.

We met with Karen, Jeffrey, and the videographer, Donald Myers aka Angry Gay Pope. I spent almost three hours sharing my story. Beth was also in one of the videos and explained how our friendship began when we met in our early twenties as we were both working at Bob's Big Boy. I told her after we became friends that I was a Scientologist, but I never pushed it on her. In fact, I never pushed it on many of my friends and chose not to tell most of them. Beth told me in later years that she wanted to tell me it was a bad organization, but she had a feeling she should just keep quiet. Beth tries hard to help me reconnect with my kids and gives me lots of strength to keep fighting for them.

My story was quite detailed and ended up being five different videos. Search YouTube Lori Hodgson Scientology to watch the "Surviving Scientology" Lori Hodgson videos. I owed a big thank you to Karen de la Carriere; my interviewer Jeffrey Augustine; Donald, the videographer; and Beth, for helping me share my story. There were thousands of YouTube hits for my videos. I was so thankful that I could help educate other people on how Scientology recruits children and how this cruel, heartless organization broke up my family. I never would want that for any family and that is why I spoke out. I wanted more than anything for my family to be back together again and for disconnection to stop once and for all for everyone.

After Beth and I finished up our day with the video interviews, we had dinner with Jeffrey and then we headed to Malibu for a few days. Beth had an uncle and aunt living there and they invited us to stay with them. I'd never been to Malibu so it was a real treat for me. We had a great time.

I made another big attempt that July to try to get my kids back: an open letter to the leader of Scientology, David Miscavige. I shared my open letter with Tony Ortega and he shared it for me on his own blog now. Tony left the *Village Voice* and started his blog, "The Underground Bunker," tonyortega.org.

I had heard David Miscavige regularly read Tony's blog so I was hoping he would read my open letter. I shared the link to the letter on my Twitter and Facebook page and shared it on several of Scientology's Facebook sites. Here is my letter:

David Miscavige,

My name is Lori Hodgson. I am a mother to two adult children, Jessica and Jeremy Leake.

I resigned from The Church of Scientology on August 30, 2010. Because I spoke publicly about the abuses that my children and I endured, the church, under your authority, applied its "disconnection" policy, tearing apart our family.

"Disconnection" is a policy written by Scientology's founder, L. Ron Hubbard. He later appeared to cancel it, but the practice never actually stopped. And now it appears you've taken its cruel effects to a more destructive level.

I'm appealing to your sense of decency as a human being. How would it feel to have those dearest to you taken away? Imagine being ripped apart from those you love most. This is what disconnection does.

You lead a group that claims to be the most ethical people on the planet, yet you're responsible for splitting apart so many people.

I hold you responsible for breaking up my family. I have been disconnected from my daughter Jessica and my son Jeremy since Feb 6, 2011. I miss my children terribly and what you have done is beyond cruel.

> *I'm not only speaking for my own situation, but for all of the families that have been destroyed by this practice.*
>
> *I'm asking you to find some human decency within yourself to end disconnection once and for all.*
>
> *All you have to do is make one phone call to your executives and tell them you've called off the policy and that you'll allow disconnected families to reunite again.*
>
> *Please do what is right.*
I await your reply.
Lori Hodgson

I knew I would probably not hear back from him, but I gave it a shot and at least Miscavige knew I was a mom fighting hard for her kids.

Later that summer, I heard that the actress Leah Remini had left Scientology and her family left with her. I reached out to Leah's sister Nicole on Facebook and shared my disconnection story with her. She responded and asked if she could share my story with her family. I said, "of course." Nicole got back to me and said they were all very sorry about my losing my children to Scientology disconnection. She and I stayed in touch and I shared with her many of my attempts to try to reconcile with my children, including my open letter to David Miscavige. Nicole was very supportive and the support I got from the Remini family was very encouraging and helped give me courage for another trip to Austin to try to talk sense to my kids. This time, however, I would be taking a camera crew.

Chapter Twenty

Working with 'Inside Edition'

After I sent out my open letter to David Miscavige and got no reply, I thought I needed to do more to help end the disconnection. I decided to write a letter to the TV networks in October 2013. Here is the letter I sent out:

> *My name is Lori Hodgson and I'm a former Scientologist of thirty years and a heartbroken Mother. I have lost my two adult children, Jessica and Jeremy Leake, to Scientology's cruel Disconnection Policy that destroys families. I am reaching out to several networks to share my story on a broader level.*
>
> *Disconnection is real and I'm currently living it with my disconnected children. I would love to have the opportunity to be on your show. My reason for speaking out is so that NO OTHER PARENT will have to go through what I am with losing my children to an organization full of lies, cruelty & abuse. There are hundreds of families broken apart due to disconnection. I also know speaking out will help me get my children back.*
>
> *I fought against Scientology to keep my children in their accredited schools so they could get a proper education. Scientology wanted something different, to take my kids from me and dedicate their lives to serving Scientology. This is wrong and why I resigned from Scientology!*
>
> *Please see my five recent videos regarding what happened with my kids.*

More Information:

Tonyortega.org (Search term Lori Hodgson for background information and updates)

YouTube.com (Search term Lori Hodgson for five-part video series)

My Story "A Mother's Heartbreak": http://aidathomas.wordpress.com/whats-your-story/

Sincerely,
Lori Hodgson

I had just sent this letter out to three networks on Friday, October 18, 2013, and the fourth place I decided to send it to was "Inside Edition." The following Sunday evening around nine p.m., I Googled their network contact info and found the link to send an email. So off it went. The next morning, on October 21, I got an email back from the Senior Producer/Managing Editor of "Inside Edition." He said, "Hi, Lori: Thanks for your email. I would like to chat with you about it. Please call me when you can at the number below."

I couldn't believe I had heard back and that quickly, too. I called my mom to share the news, walked my dogs, and then called him. He was so compassionate and said he was so sorry about what I was going through.

Bob, the "Inside Edition" manager, and I talked often over the next two weeks. I shared all my disconnection info with him. He asked me if I would like to share my story on the show from my San Jose home and they could film it in my son's room. That way, I could share how I left his room the same. I also had lots of pictures. Then Bob and I talked about the possibility of my having a meeting with my son to reconcile in Austin on a new visit.

At first, I was really excited about this idea, but I gave it some thought and called him back a week later and said I couldn't do it. I explained that if my son rejected me it would be too hard on me. Bob understood. Then I gave it some more thought and got some encouragement from my friends and family to give it a shot. It would give me a chance to see my son without Scientology interfering because "Inside Edition" said they would be able to get me and my mom there without being tracked. I called Bob and told him I changed my mind. I wanted to go with "Inside Edition" to try to reconcile with my son and end the disconnection.

Three weeks later, my mom and I were driving back to San Jose on a Monday morning because we were catching an early flight to Austin the following morning. "Inside Edition" had arranged our flights at the last minute so we wouldn't be tracked by Scientology and they also booked our hotel reservations under a different name.

I told "Inside Edition" about my earlier harassment from Scientology and how they had followed me in the past, so they took caution in how to get my mom and me to Austin. I looked on this as a once-in-a-lifetime opportunity to try to reconcile with my kids and not have Scientology getting in the way. "Inside Edition" went along so I could get there without anyone knowing and also have protection in case Scientology showed up to intervene in my exchange with my son.

Mom and I had a lot to do before our flight. We had a four-hour drive to San Jose and then had to go pick up a few things for our trip. I started packing late in the evening and I accidentally tripped on my mom's suitcase while rushing around. My toe got caught on the edge and went backwards. I was hopping around the house in excruciating pain.

My friend Beth wrapped my toe and I put ice on it. The pain was so bad that I couldn't sleep and I knew I had to get up at four a.m. to get ready to head to the airport. I had told my good friend who lived in England, Sam Domingo, about my trip and so I was able to chat with her about my toe at that early hour and whether I should cancel the trip. After she helped me look at my options, I decided not to go to the ER and just suck it up because I was not missing this opportunity to see my children. I took some Ibuprofen to ease the pain. My toe was bent back pretty bad and I just stuffed it in my shoe, biting my tongue throughout the process. Then off we went to the airport.

Thank God, no one was following us. The "Inside Edition" plan worked. My mom and I were on our way to Austin. We arrived in the afternoon and we were meeting my producer at the airport. Luckily, we got there an hour before he arrived and I was able to take some more Ibuprofen for my toe. I thought the pain was so bad I had probably broken my toe. I told Mom that I wasn't going to tell the producer that I thought my toe was broken. I decided to just forget about it and concentrate on reconciling with my children. My kids were the most important thing to me and ending this disconnection was my top priority.

We met our producer and we really liked him. He filmed us getting our luggage at the Austin airport and walking toward the exit door and our rental car. When we got to our hotel, we met for dinner. I explained my disconnection story in detail with the producer. We went over our plan to try to see my son the following morning. I woke up early. My toe was still killing me, but I had no time to worry about it. "Inside Edition" interviewed me about my story for about one-and-a-half hours.

Shortly after that, we all headed to my son's work at the motorcycle store. Joining me in the van were the producer, the film crew, and my mom. They were filming me on the way and I was so nervous, worrying whether I would really be able to see my son and hug him again, or if he would not want to see me. I wanted to see him so bad and just have a chance to talk with him again. I planned on sharing as much as I could with him this time and showing him what Scientology had said about me on the Internet. It was sexual libel and really awful. I knew my son would find what Scientology wrote about me repulsive. He would get to see what they were really doing and how they hid it with a disguised website.

The shop was about a twenty-minute drive from our hotel. Since I already knew the layout of the store and parking lot, I told them to park on the far side parking lot. As we approached around ten-thirty, I saw my son's tan truck. My dad had given the truck to Jeremy when he was sixteen for him to get to school. Dad was an awesome Papa to his grandkids and he was very proud of them with their good grades in school, so he rewarded each of them. He gave my daughter a car when she turned sixteen, too.

We parked about four cars away from Jeremy's truck, hoping he would come out for a break. I didn't want to go inside the store, so that is why we planned to try to meet with him by his truck. We sat in the van for about thirty minutes. There was one other van on the other side with an "Inside Edition" film crew. Since I had been harassed by Scientology operatives in the past, we wanted to make sure we had this filmed for my protection in case Scientology claimed something different than what actually happened and if they harassed me again. We also thought that having my meeting with my son filmed would keep Scientology away from Jeremy and me.

Scientology always tried to say they did not enforce disconnection, but if they were caught intervening between my son and me by "Inside Edition," we would have proof. I was a little uncomfortable wearing a mic, but knew it was necessary for my protection in case Scientology harassed me again.

We had our eyes on the side door and the door opened. Two employees came out, but no sign of Jeremy. Thank goodness the employees didn't notice us. We were quietly waiting and I was going over in my mind all the things I wanted to say to my son. Then I looked up and there was Jeremy coming out with two other employees. He was walking toward his truck. Now was my moment to get out of the van.

My heart was racing. I opened the van door and quickly walked up to Jeremy. He saw me and started to walk away. I followed him, saying, "Jeremy, I just want to talk to you for a minute."

I was almost running to catch up. He turned around and saw the camera guy following us and said, "No cameras!"

The "Inside Edition" cameras stayed at a distance so Jeremy and I could have our reunion. Jeremy and I hugged each other. To be able to hug my son again was incredible. I didn't want to ever let him go. I knew I might not have much time and I wanted this time to fully explain to my son why I couldn't go back to Scientology. I told Jeremy I just wanted to end this painful disconnection and be his mom again. The first thing I discussed with him was an anonymous attack website that Scientology admitted being a part of.

I told him to search for it on his phone. "Jeremy, you will see I'm not lying. Put in my name, Dear Diary, and Scientology."

He put those key words in and *boom* it showed up in his search.

I said, "Yes, that's the one!"

He read it quietly and looked upset as he read it. I think he couldn't believe that he was reading this about his mom. There was a picture of me in a boat with my friend Marty and under the picture it said, "Me taking Lori out to test her flotation devices."

I told my son this was not Marty's site but actually a fake one run by Scientology. Jeremy knew about my breast enhancement and how I had kept that quiet. He seemed angry at them for saying that. Then I told him that in that article they also made fun of my limp and smaller leg in a cruel way.

As he was reading this, something happened and I think Jeremy started seeing that maybe his mom was really telling the truth. I could tell we were talking better and more openly; then dang it! his boss needed him inside.

I said, "Jeremy, please come back and talk with me. Please!" I hugged him again.

"I will, Mom."

"Please, promise me."

Jeremy gave me his word.

I stayed outside so I was in the sight of the cameras for my protection in case Scientology sent people to stop me from seeing Jeremy. I stood out in the parking lot for twenty minutes waiting for my son. It seemed like hours. In the meantime, his boss walked by and I said, "Thank you for letting me see my son. It's been a long time since I've seen him."

He said, "Sure," and we talked a bit about motorcycles. Then Jeremy came back outside to talk with me. I was so happy that he came back out. He had his eye on the cameras that were on us. The camera crew kept their distance. I continued to explain why I couldn't go back to Scientology. He seemed to understand.

After we talked for a while in the front parking lot, we walked toward his truck and I said, "Your Nonie is here. Would you like to see her?"

"Yes!"

Mom came out of the van and they were so happy to see each other. Jeremy had a big smile and they hugged. I tried hard to hold back my tears but couldn't. It was incredible to see my mom and Jeremy hugging again. They exchanged I love you's and the three of us talked some more. Then my mom went back in the van and Jeremy and I talked for a couple more hours. We were really listening to one another and it was going great. We got to the point where I said, "So, what can we do to fix this?"

Jeremy didn't have an answer. I said, "How about if we meet with your dad tonight and we can work this out?"

Then Jeremy brought up my going to my friend Marty's and how could I do that. I'm sure Jeremy was told that Marty was a squirrel and declared an SP, who is a person Scientology despises. How could his mom go see him?

I said, "Jeremy, did you know Marty was Tom Cruise's auditor?" He had to be a pretty dang good auditor to do that.

Jeremy was surprised to hear that. I gave Jeremy nothing but truth so he could really think about this situation without all the lies Scientology had told him. Then I said, "Jeremy, it wasn't okay that Scientology made you sign a three-million-dollar gag contract to not ever say what happened when you were in the Sea Org."

"They told me everyone had to sign one."

I shook my head. "Actually, that is a lie. I have talked to many people who have left Scientology and none of them were required to sign a three-million-dollar contract."

He looked at me in shock. I had exposed another lie that Jeremy now realized Scientology had told him. We were just coming to a point after talking about things we loved to do together, like dirt biking and listening to country music, when Jeremy asked, "Mom, do you have a mic on you?"

"Yes, I had to in case Scientology harassed me again."

Jeremy suddenly got really upset and said, "You are a liar and everything you just said are lies."

"No, Jeremy, it's all the truth and you never asked me earlier if I had a mic on me. If you had, I would have told you just like I told you now."

I continued to tell him that I actually forgot I had it on because for the past several hours I was in the moment with him. But Jeremy abruptly walked away from me and called his dad. I was so upset, because up to this point things had been going great. Now he was in the back of the building talking to his father.

When he hung up, he said, "Mom, what you're doing is suppressive and not okay and you lied."

"I didn't lie about anything, Jeremy."

"You wore that because of a long time ago when those Squirrel Buster guys harassed you."

"Yes, and there's been other times."

Jeremy paused then said, "You can stay, but they all need to leave."

"It's not safe for me to do that. I'm in the care of 'Inside Edition.'"

I gave Jeremy my phone number and told him to please call me that night. I asked for his number, but he wouldn't give it to me. I knew his dad was on his way and probably other Scientologists as well. Now, when I think of this incident, I look back and wish I had stayed and confronted whatever might have happened, but I think it would have gotten real ugly, especially given Jim's temper.

As I walked away from my son, I asked him again to call. I was crying on my way back to the van. This was the closest Jeremy and I had gotten to the truth and now I knew he would be back in the hands of his father and Scientology manipulators.

We went to get a bite to eat with the producer and film crew and then went to a park so they could finish up my interview.

That evening I was still with my producer and I called Jessica. Fortunately, I had gotten ahold of her new number. She didn't answer but I told her I was still in town and to please call me and come over to my hotel so we could talk and see each other. I told her that I loved her and missed her so very much! After the call, the three of us went to dinner and my producer gave me some tips for my interviews. He said I had a big, compelling story and he taught me how to stick with the sound bytes, which were the biggest events that had happened to me. I thanked him for his advice.

Mom and I called our family to share what happened. I was torn over whether this was a good thing or a really bad thing. I was happy to have the three hours with my son and for him to get the truth. I knew the seeds I planted would help him get to a place where he could really look with his own eyes. Then I thought this might have pushed him away from me even farther. I cried myself to sleep.

My mom and I flew home the following day. I was exhausted from the emotional pain of this sad disconnection and my toe was really hurting. I went to the doctor when I got back and he said, "Why didn't you come in sooner? You have a very badly broken toe."

It was still bent straight up and hanging on by not much. "I couldn't, doctor. I had to catch a plane to see my son."

He knew my story and understood why I did what I did. Then he told me my toe would always be messed up and sticking up unless we re-broke it. It was painful, but he managed to fix it up just fine.

"Inside Edition" aired my emotional quest to see my son December 6, 2013. We did not air our taped voices because I'm certain Jeremy would not want that and neither did I, and if it was aired then we would also have to give Scientology a copy.

I am grateful to "Inside Edition" for taking me to Texas because I had three hours with my son. I think airing my disconnection heartbreak on national TV was important so people could see how Scientology ripped apart my family. People could clearly see that my son loved me and his grandma and that he was being manipulated by Scientology. That was clear to me when he told me that I knew what to do to fix this, which was going back into Scientology and doing the A-E steps. I wish Jeremy could see what the A-E steps really are because then he would probably stop insisting that I do them.

I hope Jeremy did not get in trouble with Scientology for talking with me, but if he did I'm sure sooner or later he will get sick of them controlling his life and telling him who he can or cannot talk to. What church tells a boy he can't talk to his mom unless she goes back in the church and does what they order her to do? To me, that is not a church!

I can't have my children back yet, but I can still do something and that is to educate other families on what Scientology did to my family because I left Scientology. I'm not the only one going through Scientology disconnection; there are many all over the world. I continue to speak out to help prevent any other family from going through my heartbreak of losing my children and hopefully help end this cruel disconnection for everyone affected. My husband always reminds me of this and my cause of why I speak out. I sometimes am in too much pain to speak out and thank God I have such a wonderful, supportive husband to fall back on, because he helps me get ready to fight again for my children.

My mom is a huge support, too, as she is always there for me day or night. She supports me in many ways, when I'm crying from missing my kids, to jumping for joy when I think I'm making progress with them; always encouraging me to never give up. My mom and my husband are my rocks that help hold me up. My stepdad, real dad and stepmom, and all the rest of my family and friends support me, too, and I love all of them. It really helps to know I'm not alone in this nightmare.

A few days after "Inside Edition" aired my segment, my mom and I were driving from San Jose to Clear Lake. I noticed about halfway through our road trip a black sedan with tented windows was following us. We were near Petaluma on Highway 101. I mentioned to my mom that I noticed this car coming up on us. Whenever I changed lanes, it would follow. This went on for about five miles. I told Mom to get her phone out and take a picture of the car so we could get the license plate number.

Mom was all set and that's when I decided to quickly veer over to the middle lane from the fast lane, then the slow lane. The car was still tailing us. I immediately took the following exit with no signal to try to lose the car, and it followed us. I sped up after I got off on the side road and then hung a U-Turn. The black car couldn't keep up and didn't see that I was making a U-turn. They saw us and flew by fast so we were not able to catch the license plate.

I then got back on the freeway and didn't notice the car after that. In the past, I had been followed by cars as a harassment to try to probably scare me away from trying to see my son. I think this was an attempt to scare me because I went public nationally with "Inside Edition." I did get a glimpse of the driver and to me it looked like Bob Wright, Jeremy's uncle, who was also his guardian in the Sea Org.

Chapter Twenty-one

The Last Time I Saw My Son

My mom and I planned yet another trip to Texas in 2014 to try to reconcile with my kids. We tried our best to book our flight and our hotel in a very discreet way so Scientology could not find out. I was talking with a friend who was still in the church under the radar. This person was also friends with Jeremy. I was getting signs from her that my son might see me as long as no one knew. I felt positive that I could pull off seeing my son and spending time with him. I wanted to take him early birthday shopping, out to his favorite restaurant, and watch him ride his motorcycle at the track. Just have some good old quality mother and son time and then he could spend time with his Nonie. Jeremy was very close to my mom.

We decided to go on Mother's Day again. We flew into Austin International Airport on Thursday afternoon, May 8, 2014. We got our rental car in a way so we could not be tracked, then we went to our hotel. It was late afternoon and we were pretty tired from the flight and it was very emotional returning to Austin. We planned to get an early start in the morning to try to see Jeremy at work.

So Friday morning we had a quick breakfast then headed back up to our room in a glass elevator. I could feel someone looking at us and I looked down at the bottom floor where we had just had breakfast and saw this middle-aged woman staring up at us. I stared back at her and she looked away. Then I got off on the floor to our room and told my mom that I thought I'd seen a Scientology operative staring at us, and I was worried they knew we were in town. We got ready to go see Jeremy and got back in the elevator. The lady was still in the same spot and again had her eyes on us. We decided to walk right by her to get her picture and she covered her face. We knew then that it was for sure someone from Scientology and she was watching our every move to see when we were heading to my son's workplace.

I told Mom, "We'd better go right now!"

We got our rental car and headed for Jeremy's motorcycle shop. We got there as soon as we could and it took about twenty minutes. We pulled in the parking lot and didn't hesitate this time. We walked straight in. I was as nervous as last time. My heart was beating a hundred miles an hour. We walked through the glass doors and I immediately saw my son talking to another employee. Jeremy saw me and he started to run toward the back. I ran after him and my mom followed me. I caught up to him while pleading, "Jeremy, please stop and talk to me!"

He stopped and turned toward me and said, "Mom, you need to leave!"

I told him that I had told no one I was coming and just wanted to spend some time with him without anyone knowing. That way, I thought Jeremy would not get in trouble with Scientology for seeing me and his Nonie.

"What? That's ridiculous, Mom. You need to leave now and if you don't leave then I will!"

I pleaded again. "Jeremy, please don't do this! Can I give you a hug?"

Jeremy looked upset and again told me to leave.

"What about your Nonie? She came here to see you, too."

Jeremy looked at us both and he wasn't himself. He just continued to repeat that I needed to leave. This reminded me of when he wanted to join the Sea Org the second time and he kept repeating to me, "Don't you want me to be happy? I want to do this."

In Scientology, they have you repeatedly drill what to say. It sounded like my son was coached. I knew they had found out I was going to see him when I saw the lady watching us that morning. How Jeremy was acting proved to me that they had coached him on what to say to us. My mom and I still tried to get him to talk with us.

Jeremy said, "I'm leaving then."

He took off toward the back of the store. I couldn't believe my son was doing this. Then his boss came up to us and asked us to leave. He said, "I'm very sorry, but my employee wants you to leave so you need to."

His boss had a sad look on his face like he didn't really want to tell us this. I also noticed another person in the store who was not wearing a work shirt and was watching everything. I bet that was someone from Scientology making sure Jeremy did what he was told.

As Mom and I started to leave, the young girl at the front desk saw me crying and asked what was wrong. I told her that Scientology would not let my own son, Jeremy, see his mom and grandma. She was very understanding and sympathetic. I left a present I had for Jeremy with her to give to him. She said she would.

Mom and I got in our rental car and I was in utter shock over what had just happened. I couldn't stop bawling. I had my heart set on being with my son all week and fixing this whole mess once and for all. I also was hoping that we could talk with my daughter and all of us be a family again. I was so upset leaving Jeremy's work I had to pull over to the nearest parking lot and I put my head on the steering wheel, still crying. Mom was so supportive and consoling, even though she was very upset, too. I had burst into tears and that lasted for hours.

Finally, I called my friend Tony Ortega and he could tell by the sound of my voice that I had gone to Texas again to try to see my kids. I told him what happened and he really helped me calm down. We decided not to share this awful event because Scientology won this one by most likely getting involved again in my family and manipulating my son to do what he did. Thank God for Tony, who was always there for me and understood what I was going through. He told me to try to have a good time and go visit friends. After I hung up with Tony I felt better.

My mom and I spent the rest of the evening discussing whether to jump on the next flight and go home. We ended up staying there in Austin a few more days. We called my good friends Marty and Mosey, and Mosey invited us over for Mother's Day. I was still heartbroken about my meeting with my son and had a difficult time being right there in Austin so close to my kids, but so far away at the same time.

I woke up early Mother's Day morning and Mom and I decided to stop by my daughter's house on the way to our friends. I had managed to get her address and we MapQuested our route. I wrote out a little note beforehand in case she wasn't home. I wrote the address where I was staying in Austin and my phone number. My message said, "Hi Jessica. I'm in town and would love to see you. Please call me. I love you!"

We found my daughter's house, parked the car, and walked up her walkway. Mom was right next to me and we didn't notice anyone tailing us. I knocked on the door and her boyfriend, Jonathan, answered the door. I said, "Hi. I'm Jessica's mom. Can I please see her?"

With sad, downcast eyes, he said, "I know who you are and I'm sorry, I can't let you see her."

"Okay, please tell her I love her and miss her so very much."

He said he would and I gave him my note for her and asked if he would give it to her.

"Yes, I will!"

At this point I hadn't seen my daughter since the time in the hospital when Jeremy had his motorcycle accident, October 2011. I was hoping for a miracle on this Mother's Day morning that I would be able to hug my daughter again.

We got back in the car and drove off. I had a hopelessness about me that I can't even describe. It felt like I got run over by a truck, over and over again. This disconnection felt like dealing with the loss of death but in a way, it was worse. My children were alive and Scientology was keeping us apart. It was beyond awful!

My mom and I headed to Marty and Mosey's. We tried to have a good time together, but we were pretty depressed. On our way back to our hotel, we just couldn't stop thinking of the kids. We tried to think of more ways to see them and end the disconnection and decided to send Jessica flowers. I looked online for an Austin florist. I picked out a beautiful bouquet of flowers with a balloon that said "I Miss You." We had them delivered the following day. I never knew if my children received any of my presents, but I do know I sent them and hopefully they received them and knew I was always thinking of them.

While we were still in town, we found out our friend Mike Rinder was there too, so we were finally able to meet him in person at an Austin coffee shop. Mike was the former senior executive of the Church of Scientology International and worked hand-in-hand with Miscavige. He left Scientology before we did. We had a great visit. Mike is a great guy and we enjoyed visiting with him.

We also met with our friend Derek Block. He came over to our hotel and we had a wonderful time over dinner. Derek had lost his parents due to Scientology disconnection. My heart went out to him. We exchanged stories and had a good visit. It meant a lot to meet both Mike and Derek in person.

We packed our bags and the next day dropped our rental car off at the Austin airport. While we were waiting for our flight, I told my mom that I couldn't do this anymore. I meant traveling to Austin and being rejected by my own kids. It was the most painful experience a mother could have. I said, "Next time I come here is going to be when my kids want to see me."

During the whole flight home we were both very quiet; my mom could see I was really down. For months following that last trip to Austin I was still depressed. I felt like I would never see my kids again. I tried everything for them to see I wanted to make things better, but nothing worked. I felt like giving up on the situation. So, I backed off from all media opportunities.

When the summer of 2014 rolled around and it was the kids' birthdays, I still sent presents, hoping they could keep them and hoping they saw how much I was thinking of them. *They must know how much I love them*, I thought.

Right after my mom's July 4th birthday, I found out through a resource that Jeremy had quit his motorcycle job and went to work for his dad doing construction. I also found out he was back taking classes with Scientology in the evenings and weekends. When I found out this news, my heart dropped and I felt like our relationship no longer had any hope. Now that Jeremy was back in the hands of Scientology and not being around other friends that were not Scientologists, like when he worked at his motorcycle shop, he was going to get more controlled. This was the worst thing to have happen.

A few days after I heard this news, I decided to call the motorcycle shop and asked to talk to his boss. I said, "I heard Jeremy just quit and I wanted to let you know that I heard he loved his job but I think he was pressured by Scientology and his father to quit."

His boss told me that they really liked Jeremy and he was a good employee and he felt like there was an outside source influencing him to quit. I thought to myself that wow, someone on the outside who was not a Scientologist could see the coercion. I then asked the boss if the presents I had sent to his work for the past two years were still in the back office. His boss said they had Jeremy take them. I was relieved that he took them and was hoping just maybe he would open them. I also told the boss I had just sent him a letter and could he please see that Jeremy got it. His boss, who had asked me to leave just a few months before this conversation, said he was really sorry about Jeremy and me, that it wasn't right, and he hoped it got better.

Now that Jeremy wasn't working there, I had no way to reach him. I felt even further from my son than I'd ever been. During my attempts at reconnection, there were several times I felt like my son was going to turn around and say he couldn't do this any longer and then we could help Jessica see the truth. Now I felt like I had hit a brick wall and there was no detour around it.

I got through the summer trying to keep my mind on happy things like spending time with my family boating, riding my motorcycle, going to the wineries with my husband, and spending time with my mom. Every time Mom and I would hang out, we talked about the kids. She always had a way for me to look at the bright side and to keep the faith that we would all be a happy family again.

In December 2014, I decided to speak out again. My husband encouraged me to keep at it. He told me that he noticed that when I was doing something about the disconnection situation I was happier. He said, "Remember what you told me? You said, at least I can educate others about this cruel disconnection so no other parent has to go through what I'm going through."

When CR reminded me of that, I got my strength back so I could continue to speak out. It had been six months since I had made a public statement. I knew I had to do this for my kids and all the other broken families that had been ripped apart by Scientology's disconnection policy.

I had the opportunity to be on "The David Pakman Show," a nationally syndicated progressive talk show on TV and radio. How this happened was that I saw on Facebook an interview with David and Marty. I decided to email David and tell him that I was the first one visiting Marty when the Squirrel Busters arrived, and how two of the Squirrel Busters followed me from my hometown and how those two men were deeply involved in my disconnection with my kids. David immediately emailed me back and we set up an interview for the following week.

I was back at my San Jose home to do our Skype interview. There was no preparation. It was an interview where I just answered his questions. I wasn't sure if I was going to break down crying or if I could hold it together. It went well, however, and I felt composed. David put our interview on YouTube and it soon had over ten thousand views. I thought, *well, at least a lot more people know the truth about how Scientology recruited young children and ripped families apart.*

Another Christmas without my kids came and went. For some reason, I thought just maybe my kids would wake up and show up for Christmas. I had no idea why I even imagined that, but I did. My expectations were high and I was extremely disappointed again. I sat there at the Christmas table holding back my tears and missing my children terribly. When I saw the two empty chairs which used to hold the presence of my sweet Jeremy and Jessica, I had this awful misery in my heart.

Chapter Twenty-two

Fourteen National Radio Shows

The year 2015 started out with a bang. Alex Gibney's documentary "Going Clear: Scientology and the Prison of Belief" premiered at the Sundance Film Festival on January 25. Some of my ex-Scientology friends were in the movie: Sara Wright Goldberg, Tom DeVocht, Mike Rinder, and even Tony Ortega. I felt this documentary was going to help a lot to expose the truth about Scientology and that my kids might hear about it and that would bring them much closer to coming home.

In March, the two-hour documentary got a theatrical release so it could qualify for the following year's Academy Awards. I heard it was playing in San Francisco at The Presidio, so I got three tickets for my husband, stepdad, and me. When we arrived, a few people came up to me who had heard about me on Tony Ortega's blog, "The Underground Bunker," and must have seen a picture of me there since Tony had shared many of the times I'd tried to see my kids. The people said that they were sorry about me and my children and they hoped that I got reunited with my family soon.

CR and my stepdad couldn't believe that these people had heard of me. I also met two former Scientologists that I knew from being Facebook friends, Ronn Stacy and Mark Secosh. They both were really nice and I was so happy we got to meet in person.

We thought the documentary was fantastic. I knew it was going to do well and I was so proud of everyone in the movie for speaking out and sharing their experiences. The world-at-large needed to see what really went on behind the curtains of Scientology. At the end of the documentary, my friend Sara

Goldberg shared the story of her disconnection with her daughter and granddaughter because of Scientology's forced disconnection policy and tears rolled down my face. I looked over at my husband and saw his tears, too. Sara's part really got me as I was a mom in the same situation and it's one of the most painful heartaches a parent can go through.

On March 29, 2015, "Going Clear" aired on HBO. I was in Hawaii for my brother's wedding during the airing so I had my mom tape it. But the day it aired, reporter Tony Ortega asked me if I would like to make a comment for an article he was writing. He asked, "What does it mean to you that this documentary is reaching such a large audience today?"

I replied, "I am so excited for the documentary to air. It's going to reach so many people, and they will see the real truth about how Scientology destroys families. Thank you, Alex Gibney, and everyone in the documentary, and HBO. I hope my Jessica and Jeremy get the chance to watch it."

My two-week stay in Hawaii was fun but I longed for my children. They would have loved to be there for their uncle's wedding. This was my third trip to Hawaii since the disconnection that my children couldn't go on. We had always talked about how we were going to have a family trip together in Hawaii, but they missed out on all of them.

In April 2015, my friend Sara Goldberg emailed me an idea that she had. She said that her friend Marsha Friedman, the CEO of EMSI Public Relations, thought I would do well on national radio shows. They also asked Claire Headley, Cindy Plahuta, and Mary Jane Barry. I jumped at this incredible opportunity to spread the word worldwide about Scientology's brutal disconnection policy.

We one by one wrote up our stories and each of us had our own subject to discuss on the radio shows. Mine was called "How Scientology Rips Apart Families." I'd never done radio shows before so my first one was difficult for me, but as I continued, they got easier and easier. All my hosts were very nice and compassionate about my family's situation. We originally were going to just do the radio shows for the month of May, but they did so well that we carried them into July.

These are a few of my favorite shows I did:

One of my shows aired for an hour and it was with Dr. Pamela Brewer, a psychotherapist and a wonderful, compassionate woman. I really enjoyed our hour together. She wanted to start at the beginning when I was a little girl. She really helped me look at my life deeply and by doing that I was able to do a better job at writing my story.

When I was in Scientology, I heard how awful psychologists and mental health people were. How wrong was that viewpoint that Scientology preaches! I met many wonderful people in the mental health field that truly care about people, just like Pamela. I told her I was writing a book and she asked me to please come back on her show so we could discuss my book. Her show is called MyNDTALK on Blog Talk Radio WPFW 89.3 FM.

I was on "The John Fugelsang Show" on Sirius XM Satellite radio, which had twenty-seven million subscribers. John was an excellent host and he asked me great questions. He said he had heard of my story and was excited to have me on his show. All my radio shows were cold interviews. I had no idea what questions I was going to be asked. It actually was not as hard as I thought it would be. My husband always gave me great advice. He said, "as long as you stick with what you know then you will be fine." Those words came in handy many times.

"The Josh Tolley Show" on Genesis Communications Network was another of my favorites. Josh was compassionate and I felt like he could feel what I was going through. After our interview, he made it into a YouTube video and I was happy more people out there could hear it.

Another one of my favorite radio shows was with host Kacey of "SHINE ON! Kacey's Health & Happiness Show," on 100.7 WHUD from New York. Kacey asked me if I wanted to say a message to my children. That meant so much to me that she cared that much to ask me that. I hope one day my kids can hear that message and all my other messages and ways of trying to let them know how much I love them and miss them.

My last radio show in June never aired. Minutes before I was on, I usually got a call from the host. No call and several minutes past the air time I listened to the radio station and the host was talking about some other topic. I was confused so I called my radio manager. They didn't know what had happened as they had no cancellation. They called the radio station and wow, it was crazy. The station told my manager that the host could not do the show because if he did, he would lose his friend.

We found out that his friend was a Scientologist so he couldn't do the show with me or he would lose him as a friend. So the host decided at the last minute not to discuss that topic. I had heard from my manager that the host had had some experience with disconnection and was very interested in having me on his show.

These kinds of things happened to me more often than not. An important point was that this particular radio show aired in Houston, Texas, so close to my children in Austin. I tried putting those pieces of the puzzle together.

I enjoyed listening to Claire, Cindy, and Mary Jane's radio shows. All four of us who did the shows had our families ripped apart by Scientology's disconnection and we spoke out to help put an end to this abusive practice so we could all have our loved ones back. We wanted disconnection stopped so no other families had to suffer like we did.

The following week after my last radio show was my son's twenty-second birthday. I was able to get his new phone number and sent him this text message:

> *Happy 22nd Birthday Jeremy!*
> *I made you a Happy Birthday video. I love you, son, and miss you terribly! I hope we can be together soon.*
>
> *Love Always!*
> *Your mom*

I'm not sure if he received my message and video. My mom and I sent him some presents to my daughter's address, hoping he was still living there.

Chapter Twenty-three

Jessica Gets Engaged

It was Sunday morning, June 28th, and I was just getting up to have a cup of coffee. First thing I did every morning over a cup of coffee was look on Facebook and check Tony Ortega's new post for the day. As I looked at my page, I saw I had a message from a friend. I only got halfway through the message before I broke down in tears. I walked outside and was bawling so hard that the neighbors probably heard me. I went back inside and continued to read the message. I had just found out that my daughter Jessica was engaged to her boyfriend, Jonathan.

Jessica had met Jonathan when she moved to Austin. I don't know any specifics on how they met. I just found out through some friends that she had a boyfriend. I had such strong mixed emotions. I was so happy for her, but at the same time filled with an immense sadness because we couldn't celebrate this wonderful news together. I had been through a lot with this whole disconnection heartache, but this hit me the hardest.

When Jessica was younger we used to talk about her wedding. I remember after she was in CR's and my wedding, she absolutely loved it. She loved my dress and loved helping me plan it. I asked her if she would like a big wedding one day and she said yes. When she was about eighteen or nineteen and dating Justin, we had talked again a little about her wedding. That's why it was such a shock for me when she was recruited for the S.O. and she and Justin were going to have to quickly get married so they could be together in the Sea Org.

After all the times we had talked about her special day and celebrating with her family, for her to have to have a fast wedding away from all of us was just awful and I knew she really didn't want that. Then she and Justin were separated when they both left for the Sea Org and after they both routed out and came back home they got an apartment together and we started talking about a nice wedding again. We even talked about her getting married at her Papa's house at the lake or in our beautiful backyard here in San Jose or at the beach in Santa Cruz. We spent several conversations talking about the special day she would have one day.

This was one of every mother-daughter joys in life. Except my daughter was robbed of this magical time together because of Scientology. CR woke up and saw me sobbing so hard he didn't know what was wrong. When I told him, he held me for a long time. Thank God I have him. I then called my mom and my voice was quivering so hard she couldn't understand me. As soon as I got my breath, I told her and she was sad, too. My mom and I had gone through so much heartache together and here it was again.

After this news, I was quiet for weeks. I was sunken inward, didn't feel like doing much, and kept my thoughts to myself. The one thing I do when I'm depressed about my kids is work out. Going to the gym helps me feel better. A good hard workout is my therapy. So I did that, but it was about all I did.

A few weeks later, my good friend Cindy Plahuta called. She is a mom like me suffering from being disconnected from her daughter. She asked me if I would like to come for a visit and stay at her house to celebrate Tony Ortega's new book, *The Unbreakable Miss Lovely*: *How the Church of Scientology tried to destroy Paulette Cooper*. Cindy was throwing him a big celebration barbecue. I told Cindy I would love to. She cheered me up and I thought what better way to get me back up fighting for my kids again than to be with great friends all fighting the same cause. I told her yes, I would be there and asked if I could help with the party. I was excited to meet Cindy in person and to meet Tony Ortega, too, who had been writing about my disconnection story since Jeremy's bad motorcycle accident back in October 2011.

In the meantime, one week before my trip to Cindy's, I decided to start my own blog. I called it "A Mother's Heartbreak." I had considered doing a blog for quite a while and with the news of my daughter's engagement there was no better time to write my first entry about her engagement. One of my Facebook friends helped me with starting the blog a few years back, but I wasn't ready at that time to stay with it.

Here is my first blog entry written on July 9, 2015:

> *"My Jessica is engaged…*
>
> *…and I'm truly happy for you. Congratulations to you and Jonathan!*

I found out last week that you were engaged. When I first heard the news, my heart dropped with the thought of not being able to share with you this special time of your life and I felt very sad.

Scientology has ripped apart our family for the past five years because of their enforced disconnection policy and now we can't even be together during this memorable time. I cried for days thinking about how you and I are missing out on all the exciting mother-daughter things we could be doing together such as planning a fabulous engagement party, picking out your beautiful dress, the wedding invitations, just to name a few. I will miss this time with you, Jessica…I really will!

Instead of staying sad, I'm grateful that you have found someone you love and want to spend your life with. I met Jonathan last year when I attempted to see you on Mother's Day. He was very kind to me even though we're all going through an extremely difficult situation. I thought he was quite handsome, too. I wish you and Jonathan the very best and many years of happiness together. I think you and Jonathan make a wonderful couple.

I'm sending my love to you both and remember I'm always here for you.

Loving you always!
Love, Mom
XOXO

I shared my blog on my Facebook and Twitter accounts. I hoped my daughter would be able to see it one day and maybe there would be a miracle and we would be reunited by her wedding day. I prayed to God for this miracle.

On July 16th, I flew to Denver, Colorado, for the party for Tony Ortega. I got off the plane and was greeted by my beautiful friend Cindy. We had been friends on Facebook for a few years so we already felt like we'd known each other for a long time. We met through this painful disconnection and supported one another.

After we had lunch, Sara Goldberg arrived. I was so lucky to have the opportunity to also meet Sara. She was also invited to the party and was staying at Cindy's. We three Mama Bears were a powerful team and we were on a mission to get our children back. Later that afternoon, we got to meet Tony

Ortega with Claire and Mark Headley and their three adorable boys. Wow! It was fantastic meeting everyone a few days before the big party.

Friday evening we all went to downtown Denver to listen to Tony Ortega talk about his new book. Tony did a great job and we had a really fun time. There was a Scientology reporter trying to get an interview with Tony.

The next day was the barbecue. I reconnected with my classmate from high school, Sylvia. We hadn't seen each other in over thirty-five years when we were both Scientologists attending a Scientology school. She and her husband left Scientology a few years ago. It was great catching up and sharing stories.

What a party! It was a blast! I brought my copy of Tony's book and he autographed it for me. I stayed for a couple more days bonding with Cindy and Sara and sharing ideas of what else we could do to speak out.

On July 31, 2015, I decided to write my second blog post:

> *"Back around the year 1998 I had a bad feeling I was in for a rough road…*
>
> *…my son Jeremy was only around 5 years old and my daughter Jessica was turning 8. I was the Preschool Director of Los Gatos Academy. The preschool was a non-denominational school, but the upper school where my kids attended was a Scientology school.*
>
> *I remember clearly this one alarming afternoon, I saw a parent crying and I asked what was wrong.*
>
> *She replied, "My daughter is leaving soon for the Sea Org," which is the elite branch of Scientology where members are required to sign a billion-year contract to dedicate their lives to work for Scientology.*
>
> *I mentioned to her "if you don't want her to go, why don't you just say no?"*
>
> *She said, "I can't do that!"*
>
> *I was confused… I said "WHY?"*
>
> *She replied, "I can't talk about it!"*
>
> *I knew at that moment that I needed to be very concerned with my own children when they reached their teenage years. I didn't know at that time that if you're a Scientology parent and you disagree with Scientology's recruiting your kids for staff or the Sea Org, that it's almost impossible to fight it. This is why this parent told me she couldn't talk about it. I found out this first hand when I had to go through the recruiting of my own children. I will go into this in more detail in a later post.*

> *That same evening, I discussed with my first husband, Jessica and Jeremy's father, what had happened with this parent and her daughter. After I told him what had occurred, I listened to what he had to say. He told me that he didn't see anything wrong with children joining the Sea Org. He thought it was a good thing.*
>
> *Then he shared with me that his ex-wife's son, Chris Leake, joined the Sea Org when he was only around 12 years old. He continued on to tell me that Chris went "over the rainbow," which is a secret place in Scientology and even his own mother didn't know where her son was.*
>
> *I told my husband that I thought that was absolutely crazy, that I would never allow our children to do that. I felt bad for Chris's mom. Little did I know...My husband was not on the same page as me. I was shocked by his reaction and couldn't think with losing our children to the Scientology Sea Org.*
>
> *He then told me that his stepson, Chris, married Roanne, who is L. Ron Hubbard's granddaughter. Shortly after this time, we met Roanne and Chris, but had to keep it on the down low. My ex was acting very secretive about the whole meeting.*
>
> *A few months later, I observed these Sea Org recruiters wearing their naval uniforms showing up on the campus. They were actually recruiting the young high school children to drop out of school and join the Sea Org. I really started worrying and thought to myself "I have to prevent this from happening with my own children when they reach high school age."*
>
> *I guess my worry and concern for my children were well justified and at that time I had no idea of the nightmare that was ahead of us.*

I shared my blog post on my Twitter and Facebook.

August was pretty quiet. I was debating whether to go to Texas again for my daughter's birthday that month and see if she would talk to me. Then I decided against it, remembering the decision I had made on the last trip —that the next time I got on a flight to Austin it would be when my kids asked me to come see them. My mom and I did pick out some birthday presents and sent them off to Jessica, still not knowing if she would receive them.

It is so difficult to pick out greeting cards for my kids, but I do my best. Reading the messages on the cards makes me upset. I often think to myself when I'm trying to choose a card, this card doesn't work or this one because I can't see my kids, let alone get on the phone and have a conversation.

That October my mom and I sent my kids a Halloween gift basket filled with some of their favorite treats. My kids loved Halloween, so I knew they would love our gift. The question was, did Scientology manipulate them to not keep our gifts? Did they have to throw them away, give them to their dad, or to Scientology?

One day, I hope I can get many answers. All I can do is hope my children know how much I love them, send them my love, and continue to have faith that this nightmare with my broken family will be over soon. I will never give up on my children and will fight for them if it's the last thing I do. I love my kids so much! My family and I are looking forward to the day we can all be a happy family again without the interference, control and manipulation of the Church of Scientology.

The beginning of November was fairly quiet. I was enjoying my favorite time of year when all the leaves are changing colors. The Sunday before Thanksgiving, I heard through a Facebook message from a booking agent for "Inside Edition." Her name was Carly and she said, "Hi Lori, I hope this message finds you well. My name is Carly and I work with 'Inside Edition.' We interviewed you a couple of years ago. Wondering if you are available tomorrow to speak about Leah Remini's book ***Troublemaker**: Surviving Hollywood and Scientology*. If you could please get back to me at your earliest convenience it would be greatly appreciated. Looking forward to hearing back from you! Thank you."

When I returned her call, she asked me if "Inside Edition" could send a film crew to my house in the morning to interview me. I told her that I was not in San Jose; that I was up at my lake house and that it was a two-hour drive to the closest airport. She said they would have to probably do a Face Time interview. I said that was fine. So Monday morning, I did a Face Time interview with one of the producers from "Inside Edition."

The producer that interviewed me was the same producer that was at Tom Cruise and Katie Holmes's wedding producing a segment for the show. His first question for me was about Suri lying on the floor crying at Tom and Katie's wedding and what I thought about that. I told him that Scientologists believe that children are spiritual beings and they can handle a lot of responsibility, but I didn't have much more to say regarding that question. Unfortunately, that was the only question they aired of my interview and I was in the middle of the segment with Tom Cruise, Katie Holmes, and Leah Remini. I bet Scientology was freaking out that I was on "Inside Edition" again.

They interviewed me for about thirty minutes and asked me about my disconnected kids and if I had any other family members disconnect from me. I said, "Yes, my stepsister also disconnected from me."

They also asked me what I thought about Leah and Katie leaving Scientology. I replied, "I'm happy they did leave because if they didn't, they probably would have lost their children like I have."

They then let me discuss the book I was writing about my children. I mentioned about how Scientology made my son sign a three-million-dollar gag contract to silence him. The producer's eyes got huge as he was interviewing me. I have a feeling "Inside Edition" will use my interview in following segments when they feel it would be a good fit for current Scientology developments.

Chapter Twenty-four

Another Holiday Season without My Children

CR and I had just moved from our little Blue house near the lake to our new Hill House over the summer and this was our first Thanksgiving in our new home. Our Hill House is breathtakingly beautiful. It's in Lakeport, but on the top of a hill overlooking Clear Lake and Mount Konocti.

I know my children would just love it here. I hope Jessica and Jeremy will be able to join us for Thanksgiving dinner one year. We had a lovely dinner and it was a very nice Thanksgiving, but I missed my kids so very much. I thought of them many times throughout the day.

On December 11, 2015, I wrote my third blog post called

> "My Christmas Wish…..
>
> *is to be reunited with my children and for all the other families to be reunited that are broken apart due to Scientology's cruel, enforced 'Disconnection Policy'."*
>
> *Scientology says there is no enforced 'Disconnection Policy'; that it is each parishioner's own choice who they want to be in communication with. This is a lie! For example, with my own children….how can it be their choice to never see their mom or grandma again unless we comply with Scientology's demands. My disconnected son told me that he loves me and wants to be with me, but he doesn't know what to do. If he sees me then he will lose his father and get expelled from Scientology. This is not*

his own choice; it is a "Sophie's Choice." This is one of the ways how Scientology keeps their members in line.

Sooner or later, the controlled Scientologist will walk away and be free again to see whomever they want and think for themselves.

I have high hopes that my children will be back with me again.

I will never give up on my son and daughter.

Think about it, Jessica and Jeremy. Isn't FREEDOM, LOVE and FAMILY a much better choice?

Love Always,
Your Mom

I shared my blog post on my Twitter and Facebook in hopes that my children would see it somehow. I also sent it to Tony Ortega and said he could share my new blog post on his blog. He shared it on "The Underground Bunker" the following morning.

My mom and I sent Jeremy, Jessica, and her fiancé Jonathan "Mrs. Prindables Apples" for Christmas. My kids loved these caramel-coated, chocolate-sprinkled apples. I used to get them for Christmas and we all enjoyed them. I know they would love them if they were able to keep our present.

Around the 15th of December I decorated my tree. I had saved many of the Christmas decorations my kids made me and was reminiscing over them. I came across my kids' first Christmas ornaments and wished Jessica and Jeremy were here decorating the tree with me. I took a picture of Jessica's first baby ornament and shared it on my Facebook in hopes that she somehow could see I was thinking of her. There is never a day that goes by that I don't think of my kids and how much I miss them, but this Christmas season I was feeling a little more positive about our reconnection than the previous ones without my kids. Maybe the positive feelings I was experiencing were a sign that next Christmas my family would be back together again.

Our Christmas Eve was nice. We had my mom, Val, and my stepson Peter over and CR barbecued a yummy prime rib. It was a wonderful family Christmas celebration with the five of us and next year I prayed there would be the presence of my children sitting around the dinner table celebrating Christmas with us. Jessica and Jeremy spent twenty Christmas Eves with our family and I knew they missed these fun family times very much.

On Christmas Day, my husband and I drove to San Jose to spend the day with my dad, Leanie, and family. My dad and Leanie's home is where my kids and I also spent twenty Christmases. Jessica and Jeremy always looked forward to Leanie's delicious Christmas Day dinner. She made these incredible raviolis that Jeremy could never get enough of. We always took home leftovers. Unfortunately, because of Scientology we had been robbed of the last five Christmas days together. We had a wonderful Christmas Day, but for me the sadness of not having my children with us left a big hole in my heart.

Chapter Twenty-five

"20/20" and "Good Morning America"

In March 2016, my mom and I were driving back to San Jose when I got a message from Dan Koon who was a Facebook friend of mine. We connected through mutual friends that had left Scientology. He asked me if I would be interested in an excellent opportunity to forward my campaign to reunite with my kids. He called me later that day and we discussed it further.

I was asked to join some of my friends and participate in an interview with "20/20" on ABC. A few weeks later, producer John Bentley contacted me and interviewed me over the phone. After the interview, John asked me if I would like to do an interview with "20/20". He was very compassionate and felt very sad about my disconnection with my kids. He said, "'20/20' would like to be able to give you a platform to get your story out there." I said yes and thanked him for asking me.

On April 12th I flew to LA for the interview. My friend Skip Press met me at the airport with a driver from "20/20". I didn't want to go by myself because in the past I had been harassed by Scientology.

We held the interview in a nice hotel in LA. There were seven of us on the panel and we were all interviewed. It was very emotional for me hearing so many sad stories. I had to hold back my tears; it was tearing me up inside. I was the fifth one to be interviewed and totally exhausted. It was about four p.m. when I took a break. I thought I couldn't do it due to hearing the other stories. I was emotionally exhausted. Then I got my strength back and was able to do my interview. The main thing I stressed was a message I had for David Miscavige, the leader of Scientology, telling him to give me back my kids and let all the other families be reunited. Out of everything I shared, this was my goal—RECONNECTION FOR ALL!

We finished my interview around five-thirty and a driver from "20/20" drove me back to LAX to catch a flight back home. I had a couple of hours until I boarded so I got some dinner at a pub at the airport. While I was on the phone with my husband, I noticed a man staring at me. He was probably a private investigator from Scientology trying to intimidate me for speaking out again. I was used to that so I ignored him and kept my conversation going with my husband about our weekend plans and said nothing about my interview. I got home late and was completely wiped out. It had been a long day.

On April 29th, John Bentley emailed me that I would be on "20/20" that evening, but that I was only on briefly. He said that "Nightline" on ABC was very interested in my story and decided to air it that evening. My mom, stepdad and my husband were all sitting with me ready to watch "20/20". After it was over, we had an hour to wait until "Nightline" aired. I got a call from my dear friend Cindy Plahuta from Denver. Our times were different because she was on Mountain Standard Time and I was on Pacific Standard Time. She said she was watching "Nightline" and that my kids were on it. I was absolutely shocked.

"What do you mean?" I asked.

She said that she had just finished watching Jessica and Jeremy on the show. I asked her to rewind it and tell me what they said. She said it was awful and that maybe I shouldn't watch them.

I said, "it's okay, what did they say?"

She told me and I was numb. I couldn't believe what Cindy was telling me. I thanked her for giving me a heads up and I waited for the airing so I could see my kids. When I watched them, I couldn't believe they said the things they did. I was really hurt by their words. I thought that both my kids looked suppressed and not themselves. I felt like they were just reading a rehearsed script with no emotion. Here are the words in their interviews:

> *Jeremy: "She keeps going to the media and putting our personal information and our life for the world to see with, you know, false information, and which is gonna upset us."*

> *Jessica: "I don't believe that she really wants a relationship with me. I think it is more important for her to have this vendetta against my church than to have a relationship with me."*

I was up all night after that double whammy and was replaying their words in my mind over and over. The next morning I wrote to John Bentley, the producer of "20/20" and told him that I was really surprised that my kids were on "Nightline" and that I had no idea they would be on that show.

He tried to explain what happened. "The church sent the videos of your kids at the last minute and we needed to air them so they were put on 'Nightline' along with your segment." He added that "Scientology had Monique Yingling, a Scientology attorney, go on '20/20' at the last minute and she took a lot of our air time and that is why your other part and all the others from the panel were cut."

That morning, my kids and I were on "Good Morning, America" on ABC. It was the segment that was shown on "Nightline" the previous night.

Over the next few days, I was still in shock. On Monday, I had a radio show that I agreed to do a few weeks back and I wasn't even sure I could keep it together to do the show. I did do it, however. It was "Shine On! The Health & Happiness Show" with host Kacey. I had done a previous show with her. We discussed the interviews that my kids were manipulated to do and discussed that Mother's Day was coming up soon. She let me say a message to my kids, which I did with my deepest love for them. I shed tears throughout the radio show and it was one of the hardest things I had to do, but it helped me to talk about what I was feeling.

Chapter Twenty-six

My Daughter's Wedding

Jessica got married on May 14, 2016. The morning of her wedding I was feeling heartbroken that I couldn't be there with her to share in one of the most special days of her life. I grieved for hours then I decided to tweet this:

> *Dear Jessica, Happy Wedding Day! Wish I could be with you on your big day.*
>
> *Love Always,*
> *Your Mom XO*

I posted a picture along with my message. It was a picture of Jessica and me with our arms around each other, so happy before the disconnection. Then I shared that tweet on my Facebook page. All my friends and family were very compassionate and wished my daughter well in her new life with her husband, Jonathan.

After a couple of hours, I looked at my Twitter and I saw that Leah Remini responded to my tweet about my daughter's wedding. Leah said, *"Could u imagine missing your daughter's wedding bc of "church" policy of #Disconnection #ScientologyDisconnection"*

I couldn't believe that Leah saw my tweet and her support meant the world to me. Many of her friends responded to my tweet and now I had even more support from Leah and her wonderful friends.

I never thought when I had my sweet daughter that one day I would not be able to go to her wedding because of a "church."

A few months passed and I was quiet and very depressed. It was just too much sadness and I was having a very difficult time with it. I decided to write a new blog post addressing my children's interviews that Scientology made them do:

> *July 13, 2016*
>
> *Jessica and Jeremy I'm hoping you read this…*
>
> *I am responding to your interviews that the Church of Scientology instructed you both to do and sent to ABC. Here is a link to your interviews that was aired on Good Morning America May 2, 2016:*
>
> *http://abcnews.go.com/GMA/video/2020-interview-ruthless-ron-miscavige-38806173*
>
> *Jeremy, this is the text to your interview:*
>
> *"She keeps going to the media and putting our personal information and our life for the world to see with, you know, false information and which is just gonna upset us."*
>
> *Son, first of all if I have said anything false, please tell me what it is so we can talk about it?*
>
> *Secondly, Jeremy, you know I have done everything to try to talk to you privately. I have called you many times and after I leave a message your phone number is changed. I've tried to send you messages on social media myself and through friends. I've even gone to Texas and tried to talk to you. Scientology always intervenes and that is why I'm trying to talk with you with the media's help. I would like more than anything just to be able to sit down with you and your sister and talk about our situation without anyone intervening. Can we please do that, son? You have my number and I would love to hear from you.*
>
> *Jessica, here is the text to your interview:*
>
> *"I don't believe that she really wants a relationship with me. I think it is more important for her to have this vendetta against my Church than to have a relationship with me."*
>
> *Jessica, I want a relationship with you and your brother. I miss you both terribly and can't believe we have been kept apart for over 5 years because of this "Disconnection." My Vendetta is against the Scientology Disconnection Policy that is keeping us*

apart and that is all! I simply want to be your mom. I don't care if you and Jeremy do Scientology and I have said that many times. I can't be your mom though because of Scientology.... I have to go back in and do the steps that are required by Scientology to be able to be your mom. I am not the one putting up the requirements. I am not asking you to give up your religion; I am just asking to be able to be in your life. Scientology is setting the demands, not me. I love you honey and wish I could just be able to say all this to you in person. Please Jessica Call Me and let's get our lives back together again. I will never stop fighting for our RECONNECTION.... I promise that!

I love you both, Jessica and Jeremy with all my heart!

Love Always,
Your Mom

Chapter Twenty-seven

Never Giving Up

It is now March 2017 and I have not spoken out nationally since my "20/20" interview that was aired on April 29, 2016. I have not done any radio shows since the one with Kacey two days after "20/20". I just couldn't talk about my situation and I stopped writing my book. The pain was too heavy. I also thought just maybe if my kids heard I was not speaking out about our disconnection they would reach out to me.

Seeing my two children on the videos that Scientology made my children do really affected me! I was in shock! I thought my kids looked like they were manipulated to go on camera and clearly the things they said looked scripted. I really shut down and was so sad for my kids and my broken-apart family.

In May 2017, I got a job working at Safeway in my small town of Lakeport. I thought working at Safeway would keep my mind busy and distracted from being so depressed about not having my kids in my life.

I was wrong. I still thought of my kids all the time. It was now August 2017. July passed and it was another sad birthday for my mom on July 4th and again we celebrated without my kids and my mom's grandchildren. The pain of missing my kids was almost too much to bear.

I decided to try to contact the International Justice Chief of Scientology. His name is Mike Ellis. I got his contact information through a friend. I thought just maybe if I tried working internally with Scientology's "justice system" I could somehow work out a mutual agreement with all parties and have my family back.

The IJC is the only person that Scientology said I could contact if I wanted to communicate with anyone in Scientology. I called him on August

13th at ten a.m. and left a message with the receptionist to have him call me back regarding my situation with my disconnected children. I also emailed him the same message.

I did not hear from him.

That evening, I asked my best friend Karla to send my children a message. She texted both my children that she wanted to see if she could help us be reunited and that I love and miss them so very much! The text went through to my daughter, but didn't go through to my son. Karla was surprised because she had not texted Jeremy before. We felt hopeful though that my daughter got the text and that she hadn't blocked Karla from the last time she texted her. Sadly, Karla never got a text message back from either one of my kids.

The next day, on August 14, I called Mike Ellis again and left a message to have him call me about my children. This time the receptionist told me to write the IJC a hard copy letter and she gave me the address. She said that Mike Ellis does not take or return phone calls so I wrote this letter to him on August 15, 2017:

> *To IJC-Mike Ellis,*
>
> *My name is Lori Hodgson and I'm the mother of Jeremy Leake and Jessica Davitt. I have been disconnected from my two children for 7 years. I'm reaching out to you because I was told you are my only terminal. I want to make an agreement that is good for my children and me so we can be a family again. I can do good roads, good weather with my children. I am fine that they do their Scientology religion. I just want to be their mom.*
>
> *Thank you,*
> *Lori Hodgson*

From my understanding of 'Good roads and good weather,' also called 'Good roads and fair weather,' it is an application that is used by a Scientologist to help stop a family member or friend from being critical of Scientology. The Scientologist changes the subject if it gets on Scientology and they talk about happy things or the weather. When I was in Scientology, this is what I was coached to do with some of my family members that were critical of it.

So, in my letter, I'm telling the IJC I can do the 'Good roads, good weather' with my children. Even though I am not a Scientologist anymore, I would do this and not be critical of Scientology with my kids. I would respect that they want to do Scientology but at the same time I would want the same respect not to do it.

On August 23, 2017, I got a letter from the Office of the International Justice Chief. I anxiously opened it. The letter said:

Dear Lori,

Thank you for your letter 15 August 2017.

If you want to get in good standing with the Church you can do the A-E Steps. Let me know if you need assistance.

Much Love,
Sofia Horog
IJC Secretary

I had a strong feeling the IJC would respond like they did, but I had to see for myself. I thought their letter was cold and brutal! I can see that Scientology will only work with me if I do their manipulative "A-E Steps." I didn't ask to get back in good standing; I clearly stated I want my kids back and to simply be their mom.

On September 7, 2017, I wrote another letter to the IJC.

To IJC-Mike ELLIS,

I am continuing on with my baptized Lutheran religion. I will honor my daughter Jessica and my son Jeremy's Scientology religion and would like the same respect back for my Lutheran religion.

I can do 'Good Roads, Good Weather' so that we can be a family again.

Please let me know if that can be worked out?

Thank you,
Lori Hodgson

I never got a reply from the IJC regarding my second letter. I emailed the IJC to please respond!

Since I didn't hear back from the IJC, I sent a postcard to my kids on November 15, 2017. I thought if I sent a postcard then hopefully they would be curious enough to read it. My postcard said:

Dear Jessie and Jeremy,

I tried working with the IJC and now they're not returning my calls, emails or letters. Can you PLEASE call me so we can work this out and be a family again?

I Love You Both So Much!!
Love, Mom

I hoped more than anything that my kids would call me. I wanted them to know that I tried working it out with the IJC and that failed. Every time I got a phone call I prayed it would be my kids. Sadly, my kids have not called. I feel my kids do love me and unfortunately they are probably afraid of Scientology. I hope one day they make that call to me and have the strength to tell Scientology that their family is more important than following Scientology's cruel Disconnection Policy. For now, all I can do is to continue to fight for my kids and other broken-apart families. I can do that by sharing my story and educating others how Scientology destroyed my family. I never want another family to go through what I have with mine.

I got my strength back tenfold November of 2017. My sweet mom had to have a knee replacement and when I was waiting for her to get out of surgery I thought of the two times I had my knee replacement and how Scientology recruited my children when I was at my lowest. I couldn't even fight back and my parental rights were violated. What Church does that? Scientology does! After my mom was in recovery I told her, "Nonie, I'm ready to fight for our kids again!"

That same week that my mom had her knee replacement, I heard from a book publisher whom I had spoken to the year before. She emailed me this message:

"Lori, thought I'd check in with you and see if you have an update about your book. We're still here, we still have time, and we'd love to help get it done!"

The timing couldn't have been better. Four days prior to her email I had just made the decision to keep fighting. I emailed her back and said "I'm ready, let's do this!"

I gave Safeway my two-weeks' notice and told them I had a publisher for my book and I was going to be working on it full-time.

I also started writing again on my blog, amothersheartbreak.com.

I shared why I was quiet and depressed the past one-and-a-half years and that I'm back fighting Scientology's policy of disconnection.

The last paragraph of my blog post, dated December 14, 2017 sums up where I'm at now: "I tried being quiet, I tried reaching out to the IJC, and I tried reaching out to my kids. Nothing works so I'm going to continue to fight for my kids by speaking out on every platform that I possibly can. I love you, Jessica and Jeremy, and I will never give up on us!"

My friend Chris Crimy has a podcast show called "Come Get Sum." He invited me on his show on December 23, 2017. This interview with Chris was the first time I had spoken out in over a year. I was honored to be on Chris's show. He has been very supportive to me and has helped give me strength to keep my hope alive to reconnect with my children.

Here is the link to the interview: http://tobtr.com/10480261

The dark times and the sad times are what made me strong and I now know that my true purpose in my life is to fight for my family. What Scientology did by breaking up my family is wrong. I have a voice and I will share it to as many people as I can. I want my kids back and nothing is going to stop me. I'm on my course with many obstacles in my way but I will prevail. I have unfinished business. I want my kids back!

Throughout my seven-year fight for my kids, my husband, CR, has been by my side supporting me. He has told me many times "you do much better when you're doing something about it!" He often reminds me of my steadfast purpose:

"Remember what you told me in the beginning of your fight: if you can't be with your kids then at least you can educate others."

He always encourages me to keep fighting by doing the radio/TV shows and finishing my book. But, at the same time, he wants to be sure I maintain balance in my life.

For example, whenever I'm really depressed over my loss of being with my kids, CR will suggest we go dirt bike riding, go wine tasting at one of our beautiful Lake County wineries, or maybe just go out in the boat for a nice ride. He also helps me by just suggesting I go outside and join him in the garden and look out at our beautiful view of Clear Lake.

He encourages me to go to the gym because I tell him that exercising on the bicycle, stair stepper, and lifting weights is one of my best ways of keeping me strong mentally and physically.

I'm so grateful for my sweet husband who continues to love me through all my ups and downs. He is truly my soul mate and best friend. I love him with all my heart!

I hope one day my kids read my book and see what I have gone through and how hard I fought to try to reconnect with them. I do know my book will help so many other people see what really goes on with families in Scientology when one member doesn't agree with them and leaves the "church."

I remain hopeful that one day my kids and I will be reconnected and happy again. I will continue to visualize my kids visiting me here at my lake home. We're all swimming in my pool, laughing and enjoying life together. I truly hope my family and all the other families broken by Scientology are reconnected again very soon.

I love you both, Jessica and Jeremy, and always will!
I'm Never Giving Up!

Always and forever,
Your Mom